Gino Barsali
Urano Castelli
Ranieri Gagetti
Oreste Parra

PISA
AND HER ARTISTS

BECOCCI EDITORE / FIRENZE

CONTENTS

* * *
© COPYRIGHT 1977 by SCALA, Istituto Fotografico Editoriale, Firenze
© COPYRIGHT testo Becocci Editore, Firenze
Photographs: SCALA (except pages 18-19: Pubbli Aer Foto)
Translation: Frances Alexander
Design: Andrei + Arcaleni
Produced by SCALA, Istituto Fotografico Editoriale, Firenze
Printed by Sogema Marzari - Schio

PISA IN HISTORY

Many centuries ago, Pisa was a vast lagoon territory where scattered groups of people lived in miserable shacks. Today, to those coming from far-away countries and continents, Pisa from above looks like a painting of times past, crowded with small houses and divided in two by the river. Here and there are splendid palaces with subtly colored façades in tonalities of yellow or pink, which seem sometimes bright, sometimes faded. The whole city is suffused with the history imprinted on its many monuments.

Many centuries ago, close flocks of seagulls, herons, plover and wild duck found in the swamps, in the forests of Mediterranean pine and in the woods of oak, as well as on the coastal beaches, a sense of nature and a world which no longer exist. In that savage time, herds of buck and doe restlessly challenged the wind and the storm, while they roamed over the plain in search of fresh water and tender grass.

No one knows exactly when Pisa was founded. When Dionysos of Halicarnassos described the arrival of the Greek Deucalion and his Pelasgians in Italy, he mentioned Pisa: and that took place four centuries before the Trojan war! But Pliny wrote that Pisa was founded by Pelops, King of the Pisans, thirteen centuries before the birth of Christ. Strabo also voiced his opinion, among all those vague and undocumented sources, maintaining that Nestor, King of Pylos, founded Pisa after the fall of Troy.

But for us the fragmentary information handed down by ancient historians can only be valued as legend and, in all probability, no one will ever know the true historical origins of Pisa. Perhaps the Greeks, or even the Phocii were the first to land in the marshy lands where, one day, Pisa would rise. The Ligurians arrived next, followed by the Etruscans. The latter subsequently developed their splendid and, in many ways, still today mysterious civilization. But, as time passed, Roman legions began to march in all directions. From the African and Asian deserts to the cold countries of Northern Europe, from Spain to Dacia, from the Persian Gulf to Britain, the name of Rome became synonymous with civilization, power, law and order.

Cities grew up according to the Roman urban scheme of intersecting perpendicular streets creating quarters. The *forum* was the city-center. In the year 193 B.C. Pisa and Rome were allied in a war against the Ligurians. In the year 180 B.C. Pisa became a Roman colony and subject to Roman law. Caesar's legions marched against the Gauls along consular roads, the same roads we still use today. Augustus favored Pisa and in his honor the city was named 'Colonia Julia Obsequens'. The history of Pisa during the period of Roman domination is united with that of Rome.

For historical convenience the year 476 is considered the final year of the Western Roman Empire. The Barbarians continued to descend from Northern Europe to plunder the rich Italian countryside. They swarmed into the most civilized cities which, unfortunately, were defenceless. These Germanic Barbarians, with fair hair and eyes as blue as blades of steel, raided the Italian peninsula as unchallenged masters of this beautiful and fascinating land. History had turned its back on that defeated and unhappy country. The Goths seized Pisa, and their domination was followed by that of the Byzantine general Narses and then by that of the Greeks. Records of this period of tragic decadence are obscure. A period of deepest decline enshrouded Pisa's monuments, her forum and her superb Roman palaces, which rapidly fell into ruin. The end of civilization had come: it was the end of law and of an organized society. Packs of ravenous wolves burst into the terrorized cities where groups of starving people waited for death as a liberation. What little was left of life and culture in Italy did not stretch beyond the walls of Ravenna, which was ruled by Theodoric and later by Narses. Christianity alone came to the defense of the hungry population and gave renewed hope to the society in complete ruin.

The Pisans, however, managed to stir themselves and shake off the torpor that gripped them. In the 7th century a new spring began to blossom, full of promises of freedom. Pope Gregory the Great commissioned from the Pisan shipbuilders a great number of ships with which to fight against the Byzantines. The Lombards ruled over Tuscany and chose Lucca as their capital. More civilized than other Germanic tribes, they did their utmost to live peacefully with the people of Latin origin. The legate and personal representative of the Lombard Duke chose Pisa as his place of residence. With the coronation of Charlemagne as Holy Roman Emperor in the year 800, Pisa began to enjoy a certain degree of independence and commercial development together with a relative prosperity. Pisan ships attempted timid sorties in the Mediterranean, the sea which they were to dominate, almost completely, for two centuries.

At the beginning of the 11th century, the four maritime cities of Italy, Amalfi, Genoa, Pisa and Venice acquired their own individual characteristics and autonomy, thus establishing the four glorious Maritime Republics. By sea and by land they fought the Saracen pirates opening up the Mediterranean to commercial traffic. For Pisa, the end of the 10th century brought very good prospects for future development. During the year 1003, the Pisans found themselves in conflict with the city of Lucca, who attempted to oppose their maritime supremacy, but were badly beaten. New successes followed: the conquest of Reggio Calabria in 1005; in 1017, the victory over the Saracen King Mugahid, who had taken refuge on the glorious island of Sardinia. Pisa became ruler of Sardinia and therefore in conflict with Genoa in her commercial expansionism. In the period from 1030 to 1035, Carthage, Bona and Lipari were conquered by what had already become the powerful Pisan State.

Year 1051-52: the great Admiral Jacopo Ciurini occupied Corsica, provoking Genoa even further. Some years later, in 1063, another Pisan admiral, Giovanni Orlando, conquered Palermo, forcing the Saracen pirates, who had used the city as their headquarters, to flee. Pisa acquired true independence and without putting herself in a position of servitude, still remained faithful to the Empire. The 'Leggi o Consuetudini di Mare' (Laws or Customs of the Sea) were drawn up by the Pisans and recognized by Pope Gregory VII in 1075. The Pisan fleet continued its expeditions in North Africa, conquering Tunis in 1088. Pope Urban II granted the city, now in full economic, political and military expansion, supremacy over Corsica and Sardinia (1092). Even today, so many centuries later, the archbishops still refer to themselves as 'Primates of Sardinia and Corsica', in recollection of the past which is unwilling to die. The first Crusade (1089-99) is for all Christendom an opportunity to discover new civilizations. Many Pisans participate in the noble expedition and their help is decisive in the capture of Jerusalem. So the century ended, with great hope for Pisa. During the next century the Pisans conquered new commercial centers on the Syrian coast, and they also obtained privileges from the Roman Emperor of the East, Alexius Comnenus. In 1114, a powerful Pisan fleet conquered the Balearic Islands from which they expelled the Moors. After two years of ferocious battles the Pisan Consuls, together with Archbishop Pietro Moriconi and the brave soldiers and sailors of Pisa, conquer Ibiza, Majorca and Minorca. Everything they loot, they speedily send to their homeland. This historic event made the name of the Pisan Republic of the Sea feared and respected by all. Everywhere Pisan ships carried with them the pride and glory of a city which was truly free, rich and powerful. In 1132, Saint Bernard convened at Pisa the council which affirmed the rights of Pope Innocent II. The city thus sided with the Pope against all his enemies; they attacked and defeated the fleet of Amalfi.

In the meantime, sporadic fighting and rivalry broke out among the small Italian states. Between 1164 and 1175 the Pisans fought bravely against Lucca and Genoa and, changing their allegiances, sided with Frederick I Hohenstaufen, whose flowing beard earned him the name of Barbarossa (red beard).

During the Crusade proclaimed by Gregory VIII and by Clement III, the well-trained Pisan fleet participated in the sea-battles under the supreme command of Archbishop Lanfranchi (1186). The 12th century ended with the war (1194) against Genoa which was a premonition of the tragedy that Pisa would suffer ninety years later. The first signs of weariness became visible in the city. Groups of people with conflicting interests organized themselves into the two major medieval 'political parties': Guelphs and Ghibellines.

Pisa promptly sided with Emperor Frede-

rick II (the grandson of Barbarossa), despite the threats of excommunication hurled at her by Pope Gregory IX. In 1241, a great number of bishops and cardinals, en route to Rome for a Council, were captured by the Pisans who, for this act, were summarily excommunicated by the irate Gregory IX. At this point the political life of the Republic became even more complicated because of the threats of the coalition of the Guelph cities, who were also Pisa's traditional enemies, Lucca, Florence and Genoa. The city became conservative: the period of glory which had seen the republican city conquering great commercial areas came to a halt. The great protector of the city, Frederick II of Swabia, died in 1250. In the war which followed his death, Pisa suffered serious losses and was forced to accept a very onerous peace imposed on her by Lucca and Florence in 1256. But the Pisan counter-attack was not long in coming.

The year 1258: The alliance between Venice and Pisa routed Genoa at sea. The fiercest clash between Guelphs and Ghibellines occurred near Siena, at Montaperti in 1260. Much blood was spilled in that fratricidal battle which was won by the Ghibelline leader Farinata degli Uberti, and therefore by the Pisans, who took part in great numbers. But when King Manfred (son of Frederick II) died, the fortunes of the Italian Ghibellines, Pisans included, declined drastically. At a time of ferocious fighting between Italian cities, the tragedy of the naval battle of Meloria took place.

Meloria, a rocky and uninhabited isle where only sea birds dare venture, rises in the blue Mediterranean just a few miles from the Tuscan coast and the mouth of the Arno. Historians note that August 6, 1284 was a sunny and tranquil day, the sea lightly rippled and with flights of sea gulls, those predators of the air, with their raucous and strident calls. The fleets of Pisa and Genoa watched each other menacingly, crews ready for battle, each knowing that the future of one or the other would be decided forever then. Each city prayed to its own patron saint: Saint Ranier for Pisa and Saint George for Genoa. The heroic action of the Pisan sailors was not sufficient to save them from a tremendous defeat. By the end of that unlucky day, the best of Pisan youth lay forever beneath the waves of the Mediterranean, and there is not another spot in Italy where the waters of the seas are so intensely blue and green as at Meloria. Perhaps too, the good God had quite a job that evening in separating Saint Ranier and Saint George who, in all probability, were having their own saintly quarrel, in the blue Paradise of heroes.

The evening of that fatal day in August every Pisan family mourned at least one who had fought valorously but without

fortune, around Meloria. The shadow of treachery still raises disturbing doubts regarding that battle. Count Ugolino della Gherardesca, considered the traitor by his city, was locked up in the tower of Gualandi and there, together with his sons and grandsons, left to die of hunger. Dante vented his anger, because of this act, against Pisa in the Divine Comedy, calling the city 'modern Thebes' and 'shame of the world'. Perhaps Dante the Florentine did not know, or did not care to know, that more than 20,000 Pisans in the prime of their youth and vigor had fallen at Meloria because of the infamous treachery of their fellow citizen.

The years passed and the city continued to decline. Guido da Montefeltro momentarily restored the fortunes of the Ghibelline city in 1293 by defeating the Florentines who were Guelphs. But Pisa was allowed to buy peace only on the condition that Montefeltro be removed from his position of command. The loss of Corsica, seven years later, was another dire blow. Pisa fell into chaos because of the conflicting interests of classes continually fighting among themselves in the city. The entrance of Emperor Henry VII into Italy gave renewed hope to the Ghibelline cities. But in 1313, Henry VII died unexpectedly and the Ghibellines mourned his death. He was buried in the Cathedral of Pisa in a sarcophagus which was made by Tino di Camaino. Unknown people still place flowers on the tomb of this German Emperor who had instilled so much hope into the hearts of so many Italians.

After the decline of the free institutions of the Commune, wlich had contributed to making Pisa great and powerful, the city became a Signoria (governed by a Lord). The first Lord of Pisa, was Uguccione della Faggiola. He conquered Lucca and defeated the League of the Tuscan Guelphs in the battle of Montecatini (1315). Then Uguccione, who had by then become a tyrant, was deposed in 1316. The della Gherardesca family became the Lords of Pisa, but they were not able to avoid the loss of Sardinia, invaded by the Spaniards between 1323 and 1326. Other families then succeeded to the Signoria. Castruccio Castracani governed as representative of the Empire, between 1327 and 1328. At his death, Giovanni Tarlati and then Bonifazio Novello della Gherardesca (1329-41) took power. This last especially, ruled the city with great efficiency and firmness. Andrea Gambacorti, in 1374, succeeded della Gherardesca, a year after the disastrous conclusion of the war against Florence. Giovanni dell'Agnello for a short time became Lord of Pisa (1364-68), leaving bitter memories of his rule. Pietro Gambacorti, an excellent governor, was stabbed to death by his cousin, Jacopo d'Appiano (1392).

Gherardo, the son of d'Appiano, went so far as to sell the Signoria to the Visconti of Milan, who quickly sold the city to the Florentines for a vast amount of gold (1405). The anger of the Pisans exploded with extreme violence, but nothing could stay the wheel of history. Pisa, surrounded by the Florentines, was forced to capitulate in the face of hunger. In 1406 Pier Capponi, Commissioner of the Florentine Republic, took possession of the defeated and humiliated city, destroying her freedom and former independence. The Renaissance had by this time become the prevailing culture in Italy. Pisa, a medieval city, found no place in this cultural climate and declined greatly. With the entrance into Italy of the French King Charles VIII (1494), Pisa had a brief moment of hope. The city rebelled against the Florentines, but after a final siege (1509) Pisa was forced once more give in. The history of Pisa from this time onwards becomes mingled with that of Florence. Alessandro de' Medici, because of his hatred for the Florentine Republic, in 1553 declared himself Duke and was hailed as a liberator by the Pisans.

With the advent of the Medici to power, the basic essence of the modern state was formed. The old idea of the tyrannic right of conquest and of the exploitation of the conqueror over the conquered was gradually substituted by the concept of a central government to which all citizens must answer. Under the Medici Pisa began to flourish once again. Cosimo I restructured the University in 1543, redirected the course of the rivers (1545-47) and established the *Sacred and Military Order of the Knights of Saint Stephen*, with Pisa as the seat of the Order (1563). Francesco I (1574-87) was not much concerned with Pisa, but Ferdinando I (1587-1609) had the acqueducts built (1591-93), and opened up a wide canal between Pisa and the sea which is still navigable

There are many traces of the maritime glory of Pisa to be found in bas-reliefs placed on the most important monuments of the city. The symbol which appears on the Pisan flags and standards is a white cross on a red background, which, together with the emblems of the other three Maritime Republics, Genoa, Venice and Amalfi, forms the flag of the Italian navy today.

today. Having lost forever its former power, the city lived on in its memories. The 17th and 18th centuries passed quite uneventfully under the rule of the last of the Medici, who had become Grand Dukes of Tuscany: Cosimo II, Ferdinando II, Cosimo III, and Gian Gastone, with whom, in 1737, the Medici line died out.

Tuscany passed to the Lorraines, a cadet branch of the Hapsburgs of Austria, with Francesco I (1737-65), Pietro Leopoldo I (1765-90), wise and enlightened reformer, Ferdinando III (1790-1800), Ludovico I (1801-03), Carlo Ludovico (1803-07), Elisa Baciocchi (1807-14); and then, after Napoleon, with Ferdinando (1814-24) and Leopoldo II (1824-59), last Grand Duke of Tuscany before the unification of Italy.

Today Pisa has slightly more than 100,000 inhabitants and 30,000 university students. It is a provincial city which has never forgotten its great past. The palaces, churches and the very streets of Pisa still reverberate with the sound of past glories. It is as though they were trying to inform today's hurried tourist of the adventures of the Pisan sailors, on their way to conquer distant and unknown horizons.

Above

The eagle was one of the proud emblems of the power of Pisa, but at the same time the city regarded the Virgin as its protectress.

Left

A 17th century fresco by Giacomo Fardella depicting the Conquest of the Balearic Islands, from which the prestigious room in the Town Hall takes its name.

Top

This painting, on the ceiling of the Church of the Knights, depicts an episode from the history of Pisa: the capture of four Turkish ships by six Pisan triremes, which took place in 1602 in the Aegean Sea. The painting is by Jacopo Chimenti from Empoli.

7

Pisa lost her independence for good
at the beginning of the 16th century.
Giorgio Vasari commemorated the final
victory of Florence over Pisa in
a fresco in the Hall of the Five Hundred
in Palazzo Vecchio in Florence.
On the ceiling of that same room
is a painting which depicts Antonio
Giacomini, a Florentine, inciting
the citizens of Florence to punish
the Pisans and their rebellion
against Florentine domination.

FROM SPLENDOR TO DECADENCE

Year 1000: The Christian world awakens to a new reality; the Apocalypse has not come, the prophecies of doom have not come true.

Signs of Roman civilization have by this time spread all over Europe in contrast to the barbaric peoples who, in the meantime, have appeared on the scene of history. Italy is divided. The Italians find it hard to see themselves as a single national entity. Centuries must pass before this will take place. Courageous men, aware of the past, begin to examine what went before. The cities, which had fallen into abandon, find new energy. Pisa is one of these cities. The old Roman colony with courage and pride develops its own economic and political independence. It is the dawn of new times; the re-awakening which discovers the surrounding mountains, the tranquil forests, beaches and marches where the savage screech of migratory birds is heard. Goths and Byzantines, Lombards and Franks have all passed through the history of Pisa. The year 1000 cancels the battles, the dispersals, the fears of past servitude and domination. The Pisans now are imbued with an internal force that will manifest itself much later in the great cultural patrimony left by the city and its people.

Unchallenged, the fleet of the free Republic begins to dominate the Mediterranean. Merchants and seamen carry the name of Pisa wherever the possibility of commerce and advantageous trade exists; they even sail fearlessly on the Atlantic. They sail along the Portuguese and French coasts. They get as far as Calais.

Year 1063: The Pisan fleet routs the Saracens of Palermo. The rich booty brought back by this expedition enables them to begin the construction of their Cathedral whose brilliant planner is Buschetto Pisano. His masterpiece, in Pisan-Romanesque, restates the motifs of classical art and stems from the ruins of the superb works of art left by the Romans at Pisa. The life of the city is animated with an economic development which can no longer be checked.

In the second half of the 11th century, Pisa takes on a definite urban physiognomy. In the 12th century the prosperity of the city increases still further. The Pisans extend their commerce and politics as far away as the coast of Syria.

The ancient fascinating cities of Tyre, Laodicea and Jaffa welcome these intrepid Pisan merchants and seamen who build warehouses and emporia, reaching as far as Constantinople. Bonanno Pisano's art flourishes contemporaneously with the moment of great splendor of the development of the Republic of Pisa.

Year 1284: The Pisan fleet is badly defeated by the Genoese fleet. The island of Meloria is witness to the death of 20,000 Pisans and the inexorable decline of Pisan sea power. Giunta Pisano, painter of melancholy Christs filled with dramatic suffering, unusual for his time, is born in the first half of the 13th century. The sublime artists, Nicola and Giovanni Pisano also stress, in their art, the drama of the decline of the city at the end of the 13th century, and actually, at this moment of great political tension, they give birth to a new form of Italian sculpture. It is the period of their greatest fame, genius, drama and torment.

The end of the 13th century: the city suffocates. Commerce and trading, which had made her flourishing and respected, languish. The Pisans call Guido da Montefeltro who hurries to their aid. In the meantime, Corsica is lost to Genoa (1300). The internecine skirmishes between Guelphs and Ghibellines become more violent. These quarrels prevent Pisa from regaining her past glory. Even Andrea and Nino Pisano take part in the clashes in their city. Nonetheless, they find the force and energy to express themselves with extreme naturalism, poetry and equilibrium. The history of the city will never regain the fascination and grandeur that it had during the splendid period of the Maritime Republic.

The spiritual perspective that the medieval period gave to architecture, made comprehensible to all strata of society the tangible reality of a new cultural world.

The Romanesque Period

This new dimension was helped along in its rebirth through the impressive classical monuments which have endured the ravages of time, as well as the destructive fury of men, all over Europe. The neighboring Arab and Byzantine cultures also made their great contribution to the development of Italian Romanesque art, especially in architecture. The history of the Romanesque is, to a great extent, architectural history. A new way of perceiving and interpreting the heritage of the classical age pervades the Carolingian architects who are frequently inspired by it. Romanesque, therefore, signifies an ideal revival of the glorious past of Rome, its civilization and history. Romanesque architecture is a firm re-evocation of the constructive logic, a meditation on how best to interpret the forms which characterize its tendencies. This architecture establishes new rules of construction based on the division of opposing forces, and on the subdivision of surface areas, hence codifying the main rules of the art of construction from the past to the present. In the consideration of European Romanesque, one is aware especially of the Tuscan architects of Pisa and Florence. In applying themselves to the solution of architectural problems, they showed great individuality and particular characteristics. Of all the Tuscan cities, Pisa is the one which becomes completely independent in searching for the plastic values and polychrome decorative motifs which characterize the building of the glorious Maritime Republic.

The search for a new art form, which had until this time been limited to the examination of classical forms from which it had derived impetus towards constructional daring, found in the Armenian and Moslem civilizations, as if by magic, its ultimate inspiration, the fascination of distant and fairy-tale civilizations. The two cultures, the eastern and the western, blend successfully in the harmonious architectural complex of the 'Piazza dei Miracoli' in Pisa.

PISA AND HER ARTISTS

Buschetto Pisano

According to Vasari, Buschetto was of Greek origin, but modern art-historians think that he was more probably Pisan. A funerary inscription on his burial place (under the first arcade to the left of the façade of the Cathedral) describes him as the architect of the construction, which was begun in 1063 and consecrated, while still unfinished, in 1118 by Pope Gelasius II. According to another inscription, once on the base of the obelisk in the Vatican and now lost, Buschetto also built the obelisk; this means that he must have gone to Rome, which seems quite probable if we examine the style of the Cathedral of Pisa.

Bonanno Pisano

Born in the second half of the 12th century, Bonanno was an architect, sculptor and foundryman. His work shows strong traces of the influence of Wiligelmo and has noticeable Byzantine characteristics.
He began the work on the Bell-tower of the Cathedral. The main door of the Cathedral was also done by him but was completely destroyed in the fire of 1595. The only remaining works of Bonanno Pisano are the door of San Ranieri at the Cathedral of Pisa and the door of the Duomo of Monreale in Sicily.

Giunta Pisano

The first mention of Giunta Pisano is found in a document dated January 30, 1229. He was listed as 'Juncta Giudocti del colle'. Hence, it is assumed that he was born at the beginning of the 13th century. We then find him busy at Assisi where he is at work on one of his crucifixes, in which he specialized, for Brother Elijah, Prior of the Basilica of Assisi. Other documents list him as 'Juncta Capitinis Pictoris'. These are Pisan records of January 28, 1241 and August 28, 1254.
At the beginning of the 13th century, Giunta became the precursor of a new style of Italian painting. The end of that

same century finds the Florentine and Sienese masters in full command of that new mode of expression. They are productive, brilliant and quick to assimilate what was new in art. It is true that Giunta Pisano was the first to introduce the Byzantine Christ in agony into Italy, without ever trying for that unreal, exaggeration of the Berlinghieri school. Already in the cross of Assisi, strong and forthright Italian characteristics appear, together with elements of absolute novelty. The evolutionary process of Giunta Pisano's painting finds its corrollary in the rigid representational sense, symbolic of the cross of Assisi as well as in the drama of the cross of San Domenico at Bologna. In the National Museum of San Matteo at Pisa, we find Giunta's work growing out of the sentiments which are his inspiration; his art is now poetic and profoundly transcendental. The evocative elements in the dramatic movement of the figure in pain are here accentuated and frenetic. The work is in full light, pervaded with lyricism and, notwithstanding its drama, peaceful. The face of Christ is austere, but its beauty is gentle.
Two small mourning figures in the Lehman Collection in New York should perhaps be attributed to this great Pisan master. In fact, given their pictorial quality, these two panels are certainly worthy of Giunta Pisano. It is clear that the greatest Romanesque contribution to Italian painting, comes from the very strong personality of Giunta as well as from the other, complementary personality of the Master of San Martino, both of the Pisan school.

Nicola Pisano

Nicola Pisano, also known as Nicola of Apulia, was almost certainly born in Pisa about the year 1220, where he died about 1280. An illustrious sculptor, he introduced the Gothic sculpture of Apulia to Tuscany. There were many French architects also working there at the time of Frederick II of Swabia. Apulia was the best co-ordinated kingdom in Italy, always ready to adapt and absorb

significant values from the classical civilization which was still valid and operative in that area. Encouraged and stimulated by Frederick II, Nicola Pisano was able, in this climate of great cultural and social growth, to develop his own artistic personality. The times were ripe for a mode of expression more in tune with the hopes and aspirations of a new burgeoning society. Future times were foreseen in which man, with all his vital energy, would be protagonist and undisputed ruler of his own destiny and liberty, as well as master of his own life.
In the period of violent strife between Papacy and Empire, Nicola persisted in his own mode of thought and artistic vision. He was animated with the burning need to rid himself completely of the formal dictates of the Church. His freedom of expression, his talent, his way of seeing, feeling and interpreting the things around him, raised Nicola Pisano to heights never reached by Italian sculptors prior to the great masters of the Renaissance.
His works, other than the pulpit of the Baptistry of Pisa, are to be found at Lucca (Deposition, in the lunette of the left portal of the façade of the Cathedral), at Siena (the pulpit of the Cathedral which restates the theme of the one at Pisa) and at Perugia ('Fontana Maggiore', with the assistance of his son Giovanni).
His collaborators were also Arnolfo di Cambio and the brothers Lapo and Donato.

Giovanni Pisano

Son of Nicola Pisano, as well as his greatest pupil, he was born about 1245. While still very young he worked with his father on the Cathedral of Siena and the 'Fontana Maggiore' of Perugia. He was Master builder of the stupendous Cathedral of Siena in 1284 and carried out many works of sculpture as well; most of these can be seen in the Museo dell'Opera of Siena (Cathedral Museum). Educated in his father's school he soon, however, developed his own independent personality. His tragic, tormented works of overwhelming intensity are vibrantly alive and his great humanity still speaks to us today. With Giovanni Pisano sculpture becomes independent of architecture: it develops in space and is based upon the upward movement of opposing essential forces, expressing dramatic emotions, but, at the same time, maintaining their fundamental balance and never indulging in pure decoration. The pulpit for the Cathedral was created by Giovanni Pisano in 1302. It is a pulsating example of his sublime, tormented and tragic art.

The Empress Marguerite of Luxembourg was buried in a sarcophagus sculpted by Giovanni Pisano in 1313. There are interesting remains of this work to be found in the Civic Museum of Genoa. We have no news of Giovanni after 1317. He ends his earthly existence after having created art works of the highest distinction. Among these are the various beautiful Madonnas in the Scrovegni Chapel at Padua, the Cathedral of Prato and the Cathedral Museum at Pisa. The project for the church of Santa Maria della Spina has also been attributed to Giovanni Pisano.

Nino Pisano

Nino Pisano, sculptor, son and pupil of Andrea da Pontedera, known as Andrea Pisano, died in 1368. He collaborated with his father on the doors of the Baptistry of Florence and the panels of 'Giotto's Bell-tower'. His works are a very personal and emotional interpretation of stylized Gothic art. Some of his works can be seen in Orvieto, in Florence (a Madonna in the church of Santa Maria Novella) and in Venice (Tomb of the Doge Cornaro). At Pisa are his famous *Madonna del Latte*, the *Annunciation* and various other works attributed to him are in the National Museum of San Matteo. An *Archangel Gabriel* and an *Annunciation* are in the church of Santa Caterina. Also in Santa Caterina is the monument of Archbishop Saltarelli done in collaboration with his father.

Tino di Camaino

Born approximately 1286 and died 1337. A Sienese sculptor of great sensitivity, he was a follower of Giovanni Pisano. His works are to be found in the Cathedral of Siena (Tomb of Cardinal Petroni), at Florence (Monument to Bishop Orso) and at Naples, where he died, (Mausoleum of Queen Maria). His masterpiece, which is the Tomb of Henry VII, is to be seen in the Cathedral of Pisa.

Francesco Traini

Francesco Traini was active in the first half of the 14th century. A follower of Simone Martini and the Lorenzetti brothers, he was a Pisan painter of great religious and civic feeling. For a long time the masterful fresco, the *Triumph of Death* was attributed to him.

He left two remarkable altarpieces with Saints Thomas and Dominick in the church of Santa Caterina. These have now been transferred to the National Museum of San Matteo.

The view from the Leaning Tower of the great monuments in the 'Piazza dei Miracoli': the Cathedral, the Baptistry and the Monumental Cemetery.

Bonanno Pisano's stylistic refinement
and clear sense of narrative
stand out in these details
from the door of Saint Ranieri,
the usual entrance to the Cathedral.

The impressive complex of the Cathedral,
seen from the Baptistry.

Right

A beautiful Crucifix by Giunta Pisano
kept in the National Museum
of San Matteo.

Above
Giovanni Pisano's powerful and at times violent expressiveness
is often softened in his representations of the Madonna
and Child. Left, the Madonna of the Baptistry; right
the Madonna in the hall of the Triumph
of Death in the Camposanto.

Right
The classicizing balance and composure of Nicola Pisano's
sculpture are evident in this Hercules,
from a relief on the pulpit of the Baptistry.

Opposite
The Madonna del Latte, by Nino Pisano, originally in
the Church of Santa Maria della Spina, is now in
the National Museum of San Matteo. It is one of the most
significant works in all of Gothic sculpture, and is particularly
admirable for the graceful and elegant pose of
the Madonna, the dynamic composition and the delicate coloring.

The Triumph of Saint Thomas Aquinas,
in the Church of Santa Caterina,
is one of the most important paintings
of Francesco Traini. In this
exceptional altarpiece, the figure of
Aquinas, the great theologian, represents
the synthesis of Truth, symbolized
by rays which emanate from Christ
and which are reflected by Moses,
Saint Paul and the Evangelists,
as well as by Plato and Aristotle.
The books of the saint irradiate as well,
but the rays do not reach the heretic
Averroës, who lies conquered at his feet.

This image of Henry VII of Luxembourg,
the Emperor in whom Dante had
placed such high hopes, is part of the
funeral monument by Tino di Camaino
in the hall of the Triumph of Death.

16

THE CATHEDRAL

The Cathedral of Pisa was built on the same spot where once a Byzantine church, dedicated to Santa Reparata, had been. But while today we admire the Cathedral which is a splendid example of Romanesque architecture, two thousand years ago rose on that spot the superb and beautiful palace of the Roman Emperor Hadrian, the same one who built the wall between Scotland and England.

The Cathedral was begun in 1063. Pope Gelasius II consecrated the church in 1118. Buschetto Pisano was its first, very talented builder; Pisan by birth, his project for the Cathedral was of a grandiosity without precedent: with a nave and four aisles intersected by a transept divided into three aisles. Beyond the transept, the edifice extends further to a presbytery, crowned by the main apse which, in its upper section, is splendidly decorated by a majestic early 14th-century mosaic. Buschetto planned the Cathedral of Pisa by taking his inspiration from classical architecture; a church with a nave and four aisles, as is often seen in Greek and Roman basilicas. The treatment of the space and the chromatic effects, produced by the inlaid stones of the decorations, may be compared to Arab motifs which combine so very harmoniously with western elements. These elements are also recognizable in the strong Lombard round-arches, which is evidence of a previous, flourishing Lombard architecture in Tuscany. The sense of rapid movement of the row of oriental bases gives elasticity and impetus to the arches of the lateral aisles. The dome is elliptical, sustained by pointed arches buttressed at the base. The Gothic-like decoration was added by Lupo di Gante in 1380.

The many side-openings break the horizontal feeling of the building which achieves its final synthesis in the main apse.

Buschetto decorated the lower section of the exterior portion of the main apse with mosaics and lozenges of eastern inspiration, especially Armenian. The entire exterior of the church is done in this style and it reaches its greatest beauty in the façade completed by another famous Pisan, Rainaldo, two centuries later. Rainaldo completed what Buschetto had started. He blended Arab and Armenian decorative motifs into the Lombard galleries. Thus Pisa, between the second half of the 11th and the end of the 13th centuries, holds complete mastery over what becomes known as Pisan-Romanesque.

The façade of the Cathedral juts forward so as to accentuate more the sense of light and chiaroscuro. These effects are brought out by the galleries which, set one above the other as they are, admirably create an effect of equilibrium, symmetrical proportion, and a simplicity and serenity which catch and hold the eye, even of those least prepared.

The Cathedral of Pisa, dedicated to Our Lady of the Assumption, is the main church in the city. It is also the most important of the entire Italian Romanesque epoch. It was built in the form of a Latin cross in Pisan-Romanesque. This style, as mentioned above, shows strong Lombard and eastern influences. These admirably harmonious and blended elements give vitality to the severe symmetrical lines. Pisan-Romanesque carries within itself a nostalgia for former adventurous voyages to the fabulous and highly civilized centers of Arab culture, where the sirocco blows hot and dusty from the burning desert and is felt in the medieval streets of the western city.

Many churches were built in Corsica, Sardinia, Dalmatia and Apulia in Pisan-Romanesque giving proof of the validity of the style and therefore of Italian civilization. Wherever they went Pisan architects, who were the worthy descendents of Buschetto, left evidence of their endeavor and, with love and passion, worked to create the buildings and splendid churches which even today can still look ahead to future centuries with a sense of self-assurance.

The Façade

The upper section of the façade is composed of four orders of galleries with 52 small columns. At the top stands the *Madonna and Child*, of uncertain attribution. On either side are two Angels and two Apostles. In the last arcade, at the left and set into the wall, in a silent poetic corner which catches all the roseate light of sunset, is the sarcophagus of Buschetto Pisano.

The three mosaics of the lunettes represent: in the center, *Our Lady of the Assumption*; at the right, *Saint John the Baptist*, by Alessio Baldo in 1467; and on the left, *Santa Reparata*. The three mosaics have been reworked so many times that they have completely lost their former splendor. It is especially true, when we think that, in 1829, Giuseppe Modena completely redid those 15th-century works and created, *ex-novo*, the *Assumption of the Virgin*. Three bronze doors, created by Bonanno Pisano shortly before his departure for Sicily in 1180, were completely destroyed in the great fire of the Cathedral in 1595. The fire was provoked by a workman working on the roof, soldering the lead plates, and had disastrous results. Though the architectural structure did not suffer serious damage, the material loss in great works in the church was immense. When this apocalyptic fire abated, the splendid works of Giovanni Pisano lay shattered on the pavement of the Cathedral. The famous pulpit was then piled up in a storeroom of the Episcopal Palace and it wasn't until more than three centuries later, in 1926, that it was lovingly rebuilt. It was placed between the first pilaster and the first column on the right of the nave as one enters the church. However, this is not the original setting of Giovanni's masterpiece. Through the centuries some of the figures of the pulpit have disappeared, only to turn up later in well-known European museums. Unscrupulous hands of certain foreigners have repeatedly dipped into the artistic patrimony of the city. To be noted especially are the superb *Maestà* of Cimabue, and the *Stigmata of Saint Francis* by Giotto, which were taken to France during the Napoleonic occupation and are still kept in the Louvre.

The Ceiling

The beamed ceiling of the Cathedral was rebuilt four years after the fire and does not really blend very well with the stern lines of the building. In the center of the ceiling, the emblem of the Florentine Medici family was placed, as they ruled over the whole of Tuscany for many years. In 1599, when the restoration of the church was begun, the ruler was Grand Duke Ferdinando I. It was this Grand Duke who decided to restore the Cathedral of Pisa completely and invested enormous sums of money in the enterprise. The total expense amounted to 85,000 scudi, a truly vast figure for those times. The three doors of the façade were also cast after the 1595 fire. The attribution of these doors to Giambologna has been proved to be entirely unfounded. It was Raffaello Pagni, the Grand Duke's architect, who designed the project for the doors, which was later carried out by various artists, according to the traditional characteristics of Baroque sculpture, with its manneristic and decadent style. The panels of the central door portray stories from the life of the Virgin, with scenes representing, from left to right, the Nativity of the Virgin, the Presentation in the Temple, the Marriage, the Annunciation, the Visitation, the Presentation of Christ in the Temple, and, in the last two panels, the Assumption and the Incoronation of the Virgin. On the door to the left, when looking at the façade, we can see the beginning of the stories from the life of Christ, with the Nativity, the Adoration of the Magi, the Temptation of Christ in the Desert, the Baptism, the Resurrection of Lazarus and the Entry into Jerusalem. These are continued on the right-hand door with the Agony in the Garden, the Kiss of Judas, the Crowning of Thorns, the Flagellation, Christ Carrying the Cross and, lastly, the Crucifixion. But the door which is usually used to enter the Cathedral is the work of Bonanno Pisano. It dates from 1180, but this stupendous work has certain characteristics which may bring to mind the modern concept of 'Expressionism'. His works vibrate with a vitality and beauty which only the colors of the dawn, or the sound of running spring water can equal. Bonanno's door represents the dawn of a new Italian sculpture. It is the breeze of a new spirit which, tenuous and delicate as a morning in spring, guides the hand of the artist in his inimitable creation.

The Interior

Entering the Cathedral through Bonanno's door, on the wall to the right is the elegant creation, the *Madonna and Child*, by Pandolfo Fancelli, who between 1524 and 1527, did this work and the *Saint Blaise*. Another, very delicate *Madonna and Child* (1518), set in the center of the holy water fount, is the work of Gerolamo Rossimini. On the left, the funerary monument of Henry VII, of Luxembourg, who died at Buonconvento on August 24, 1313, and was buried in the Pisan Cathedral, no doubt at his express wish. The sarcophagus is a precious work of Tino di Camaino, pupil of Giovanni Pisano, and had originally been placed in the apse. Later, in 1494, it was put in the chapel of the Patron Saint of Pisa, Saint Ranieri, and then in 1829, transferred to the Monumental Cemetery only to be brought back again to the Cathedral in 1921 on the occasion of the sixth centenary of the death of Dante Alighieri.

The Chapel of Saint Ranieri

In former times the chapel was dedicated to the Virgin in Glory. Now it is dedicated to the Patron Saint of the City, Saint Ranieri, of the Scacceri family. He died in 1161 and is venerated by the Pisans. In 1688 his remains were placed in the sarcophagus in this chapel with great pomp. This celebration is repeated every year on the evening of June 16th. For the entire night small flares illuminate the banks of the river, creating a spectacle which has no equal anywhere in the world. The sarcophagus itself is the work of Giovan Battista Foggini. The decoration of the chapel was done by Stagio Stagi and his brother, Giuseppe. However, the sculptures there today must be attributed to Francesco Mosca, known as il Moschino. During his excellent reign, Cosimo III, Grand Duke of Tuscany, was very much involved in the restoration of the chapel of Saint Ranieri.

The Pulpit in the Cathedral

The pulpit in the Cathedral was sculpted by Giovanni Pisano between 1302 and 1311, exactly forty years after his father Nicola had completed the pulpit in the Baptistry. After the fire of 1595, the pulpit was taken apart. Some parts of the pulpit were placed in the Monumental Cemetery and others found their way to foreign museums. In 1894, what remained of the superb work was placed in the Civic Museum. In May 1926 Giovanni Pisano's famous masterpiece was reconstructed and put back in the Cathedral. The pulpit is held up by eleven supports: two small columns, red granite and gray granite, were donations of the Italian government. Then there are two columns, of porphyry and broccatello, held up by two enraged lions killing a horse and a young deer, respectively. Also supporting the pulpit are a Saint Michael and, opposite, a Hercules with his club in his left hand; the latter is an impressive pagan figure in the context of an extremely Christian work. Then we have the four Evangelists, with amidst them the figure of Giovanni Pisano, on his knees, in the act of adoration towards Saint John. Another small figure portrays Burgundio di Tado, who is said to have commissioned the pulpit. The marmoreal group holds up the figure of Christ who preaches truth and justice, which come to us from God through the Evangelists. In contrast to this group there is another consisting of four female figures representing the four Cardinal Virtues: Justice, with scale and sword; Temperance, with cornucopia and compass; Fortitude, who holds a lion by his legs; and finally, the figure of Prudence, nude, who strongly resembles the Medici Venus. Above this most famous group is the personification of the Church, represented by a woman nursing two babies who most probably symbolize the Old and New Testaments. Truly stupendous is the central support, composed of three figures representing the three Theological Virtues, Faith, Hope and Charity, surmounted by a capital and by a 'pulvinus', both very precious. The base of the group is formed by many small figures representing the seven Liberal Arts, of the 'trivium' (Rhetoric, Dialectics and Grammar) and of the 'quadrivium' (Astronomy, with the astrolabe, then Music, Geometry and Arithmetic). In correspondence with every capital is a Sibyl. There are eight Sibyls, three of which are copies as the originals are now in the Friedrichsmuseum in Germany, who, despite their many promises to do so, have never returned them.

But, the most wonderful part of the pulpit are panels, the most audacious and most suffered over of all Giovanni Pisano's creations. Starting at the left, in the first panel are the *Birth of Saint John the Baptist* and the *Annunciation*. In the second is the *Nativity*, a delicate and poetic scene, populated by humble shepherds, who alone have the right to be present at this great event; then the *Adoration*, the *Presentation at the Temple*, the *Flight into Egypt*, moving and melancholy, and the *Slaughter of the Innocents*, whose dramatic re-evocation of a human sacrifice is full of tragedy. The arrogant and perfidious gesture of King Herod dominates this scene with a dramatic intensity which anticipates the somber *Kiss of Judas* in the following panel; and lastly, the tragedy, human and divine, of the *Passion of Christ* with his *Crucifixion*. It is obvious that for Giovanni Pisano Christ is a real man, capable of suffering himself and therefore sympathetic to human suffering. The last two panels depict the *Last Judgment*, tumultuous and frightening. The sinners are wracked with pain and remorse; the chosen are serene and ecstatic in the knowledge that they have been granted eternal salvation.

With the pulpit of the Cathedral of Pisa, Giovanni Pisano concludes the cycle of his great works. In the field most congenial to him, sculpture, he epitomized the essence of his age. A contemporary of Giotto and Dante, he met with them at Padua (1302), an encounter now famous in which they discussed the fate of their country, of Italian art and genius. Certainly they discussed literature, painting and sculpture on that occasion. But besides the questions relating to art, they also discussed the miserable conditions of Italy at that time.

In Giovanni Pisano one encounters all the grandness and misery of mankind. He takes inspiration directly from the world which surrounds him, which charges his work with the humanity and realism that only the 'divine' Michelangelo, two and a half centuries later, knew how to achieve and even to surpass.

In the Italy of Dante and Giotto, the art of Giovanni Pisano reaches heights never before attained and it speaks to the modern world, and still in centuries to come will proclaim his greatness, pride and purity, as witness to the culture of mankind and, especially, to the culture of the Italians.

The Paintings in the Cathedral

Probably, before the fire of 1595, the walls of the Cathedral were covered with large frescoes. The paintings now placed along the walls, all date from after the fire, except for those of Antonio Sogliani, Perin del Vaga and Andrea del Sarto.

The *Saint Agnes* of Andrea del Sarto is the most remarkable and is in the presbytery of the church. It reveals a steady hand, with humane and realistic feelings, work of a master who began as a great pupil of the genius, Leonardo da Vinci. Facing the Saint Agnes is a *Virgin and Child*, an

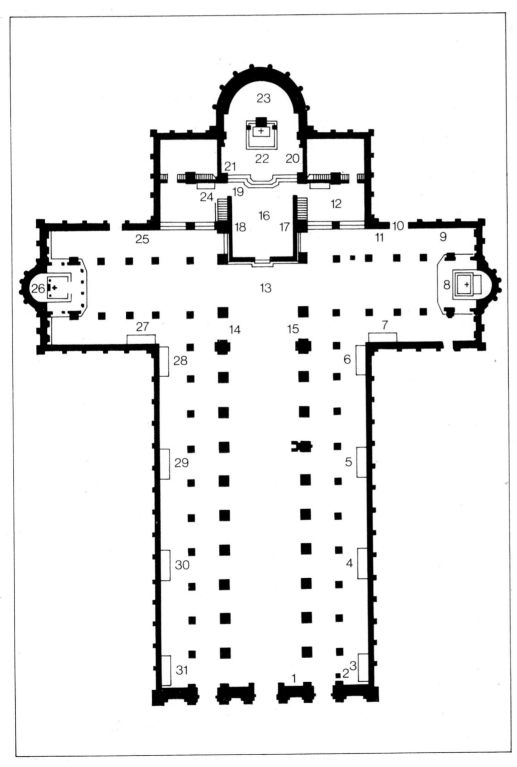

1) Tomb of Matteo Rinuccini with a bronze Crucifix by Pietro Tacca;
2) Crucifixion with Saints, 15th-century fresco of Pisan school; 3) on the altar: Virgin in Glory, by Cristofano Allori; 4) on the altar: Disputation of the Sacrament, by Francesco Vanni; 5) on the altar: Our Lady of Mercy, by Andrea del Sarto and Antonio Sogliani; 6) in the lunette above the altar: The Creator, by Bartolommeo Ammannati; 7) on the altar: Madonna Enthroned with Saints, by Perin del Vaga and Antonio Sogliani; 8) Chapel of Saint Ranieri; 9) Tomb of Henry VII, by Tino di Camaino; 10) Door of Saint Ranieri; 11) altar with statue of Saint Blaise, by Pandolfo Fancelli and Stagio Stagi; 12) Sacristy of the Chaplains, where the treasure of the Cathedral is kept; 13) interior of the dome, with frescoes by Orazio and Gerolamo Riminaldi; 14) Giovanni Pisano's Pulpit; 15) inlaid papal chair and fresco of Saint Jerome, by Domenico di Bartolo; 16) Presbytery; the two Angels on the balustrade are the work of Giambologna; 17) Saint Agnes, by Andrea del Sarto; 18) Madonna and Child, by Antonio Sogliani; 19) lectern and candelabra sculpted by Matteo Civitali; 20) Saint Catherine and Saint Margaret; 21) Saint Peter and Saint John the Baptist, by Andrea del Sarto; 22) high altar with Crucifix by Giambologna and six Angels by Lodovico Pogliaghi; 23) the apse: mosaic of the Pantokrator, the Virgin and Saint John, by Cimabue and others; 24) 13th-century Byzantine painting of the Virgin; 25) Tomb of the Archbishop d'Elci; 26) Chapel of the Sacrament with the altar by Giovanni Battista Foggini; 27) marble altar, by Stagio Stagi; 28) in the lunette above the altar: Apparition of the Virgin to Saint Ranieri, by Battista Lorenzi; 29) on the altar: God the Father in Glory, by Ventura Salimbeni; 30) on the altar: Holy Spirit and Martyrs, by Passignano; 31) on the altar: Crucifixion with Saints, by G. B. Paggi.

The complex of the Cathedral and
the Leaning Tower is one of the great
masterpieces of Italian architecture.
On the façade, the arches, which are separated by carved
cornices, glisten with polychrome inlays of precious marble.
At the extremities of the first order of galleries
are the statues of two Evangelists; at the apex is
a Madonna and Child with two Angels.
The sculpture is by the school of Giovanni Pisano.

The sides of the Cathedral have high, graceful arcades
on the lower part, and architraved pilastres on the upper
part. The decorative effect is further enhanced by the
characteristic lozenge-shaped and rosette motifs,
and by the marble inlays.

The arches and columns on the façade of the Cathedral, on the cupola and on the Leaning Tower, although they differ in style, harmonize in a unified complex which is at once plastic and vigorous, delicate and elegant.

Below
The fastigium of the apse of the Cathedral is an extraordinary stylistic synthesis of Lombard, oriental and classicizing elements. The column is surmounted by a reproduction of the Fatimite Griffon, of which the original is in the hall of the Triumph of Death.

exquisite work by Antonio Sogliani, who followed in the unmistakable footsteps of the great Raphael from Urbino.

The mosaic in the main apse was formerly erroneously attributed to Cimabue. It is possible that the *Saint John* was by Cimabue, but the *Christ Blessing* and the *Virgin*, at the left, are to be attributed to others. The works all show Byzantine influence. The severe lines of the Pantokrator are closely related to the Sicilian mosaics of Monreale and Cefalù and to those of Venice and Ravenna, the sublime periods of Byzantine mosaic art in Italy.

23

Above left

The central door of the Cathedral, adorned with episodes from the life of the Virgin, was designed by Raffaello Pagni and executed by the school of Giambologna.

Above right

The right door of the Cathedral, with scenes from the last part of the life of Jesus.

Right

Detail of a panel from the central door of the Cathedral, representing the Birth of the Virgin.

Opposite

The door of Saint Ranieri, on the side facing the Leaning Tower, is the masterpiece of Bonanno Pisano. The panels contain episodes from the life of Jesus.

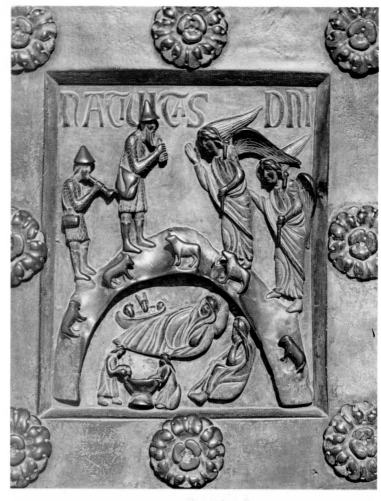

Details of the panels from the door of Saint Ranieri:
the Annunciation, the Nativity, the Procession of the Magi,
the Flight into Egypt, the decoration on the base,
and the Visitation.

Only two works of sculpture by Bonanno have reached
us intact: the door of the Cathedral of Monreale
and this door, the door of Saint Ranieri. The first shows
a style closely connected to the Byzantine environment,
while in the second, as we can see in the panels reproduced
on this page, the narrative is much more lively and
the figures are more full of movement. Bonanno does not
worry about spatial problems and concentrates all his
efforts on the characters of his stories, sometimes human,
sometimes animal, and even vegetable: for example, in the
panel of the Flight into Egypt, the donkey carrying
the Virgin or the palm-tree bending elegantly towards them
seem to be as important as the three main characters. The
motif of palm-trees is repeated in the decoration of the base
of the door. Bonanno's classical taste brings his works
to life, influencing his choice of imagery and of subject-matter.

Left
**The vast and solemn nave
of the Cathedral.**

Right
**View of the women's gallery
(matroneum) of the Cathedral,
with the characteristic orientalizing
decoration in black and white bands
and polychrome marble inlays.
One of these, on the lunette at the left,
bears the coat-of-arms of the city.**

Below
**Perspective view of the columns
of the women's gallery on the left side.**

Left
Capitals of the columns of the Cathedral with ornamental zoomorphic and anthropomorphic motifs.

Below
This view of the interior of the Cathedral emphasizes the rhythmic movement of the orders of colonnades.

Right
The left arm of the transept, with the altar by Foggini at the end.

The Chapel of the Sacrament, by Battista Lorenzi, is located at the end of the left arm of the transept. Statues by Francesco Mosca stand at the sides of the altarpiece with its ciborium, designed by Foggini.

The bronze Crucifix of the high altar, cast by Giambologna in 1573.

Bronze lamp by Battista Lorenzi, called the 'lamp of Galileo'.
According to legend, the great Pisan scientist, while observing
this lamp, discovered the law of the pendulum. Actually,
Galileo's discovery was made six years prior to 1587,
the year in which the lamp was installed in the Cathedral.

Above right
The Sarcophagus of Saint Ranieri, executed by G. B. Foggini,
is in the Chapel of Saint Ranieri, by Battista Lorenzi,
located at the end of the right transept.

Right
Detail of a lion from Giovanni Pisano's pulpit.

Opposite
The pulpit of the Cathedral
is the masterpiece of Giovanni Pisano.

Details of the pulpit by Giovanni Pisano:
on this page, above,
the Nativity and, below,
the Flight into Egypt. On
the opposite page, above,
Fortitude and Prudence and
the Archangel Michael;
below, the Last Judgement.

37

The vault of the apse of the Cathedral, with the great mosaic representing Christ Pantokrator, the Virgin and Saint John, which Cimabue was commissioned to complete in 1302, after most of the central part and been executed by Francesco di Simone di Porta a Mare and by Vincino da Pistoia.

Left
Detail of Saint John,
from the mosaic of the apse, executed largely by Cimabue.

Right
Andrea del Sarto's Saint Agnes is one of the major paintings in the Cathedral. It is located on one of the pilasters on the right side of the presbytery.

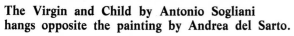

The Virgin and Child by Antonio Sogliani
hangs opposite the painting by Andrea del Sarto.

Right

Two paintings by Domenico Beccafumi, located on the lower
part of the interior of the apse of the Cathedral: Moses
Breaking the Tables of the Law, and the story of Corah,
Dathan and Abira, who, according to the Bible, were swallowed
up by the earth for having rebelled against Moses and Aaron.

THE LEANING TOWER

Few monuments in the world are as well known as the Leaning Tower of Pisa. The famous bell-tower of Bonanno Pisano is eight centuries old, since it was begun in 1173. Actually, an epigraphic inscription to the right of the entrance to the tower notes the date as 1174. That date, however, refers to the Pisan calendar which began on March 25, the day of the Annunciation. This date, therefore, predates the traditional calendar by almost a year. The tower's inclination, at present, is 4.54 meters; its height is 56 meters with an average sinking of 2.50 meters at the base. The tower inclines at about the rate of one millimeter every year and is the cause of great worry for the technicians who hope, somehow, to stabilize the famous tower permanently.

It was in 1173 that Bonanno Pisano began the construction of the tower. Five or six years later the excellent sculptor and architect was forced to abandon the work because the first signs of the sinking of the terrain manifested themselves. This is confirmation of the fact that the tower had never been perfectly vertical. The first three storeys built by Bonanno had, already in the year 1179-80, showed a certain inclination. In that same period Bonanno Pisano sculpted the four doors for the Cathedral, three of which, as we have said, have been completely lost. In 1186, Bonanno Pisano was again a long way from his city, this time near Palermo, where he was busy casting his beautiful door for the Cathedral of Monreale in Sicily.

Bonanno returned to Pisa after years of restless wandering through Sicily, which fascinated him with its classical architecture. He died in the city of his birth, regretting always that te had not been able to complete his beautiful bell-tower. The Pisans buried him in the tower. In the last century, after some excavations carried out at the base of the building, some fragments of a sarcophagus were found. On one of these fragments, which can still be seen at the left of the entrance to the tower, is the name of Bonanno Pisano. Ninety years after

Fragment of an inscription from a sarcophagus discovered during excavations near the Leaning Tower, and now placed at the left of the entrance. The name 'Bonanno' is clearly legible.

Bonanno's death, another architect, Giovanni di Simone, continued the work. Starting at the third tier, he tried in vain to straighten the tower. In fact, beginning with the third tier, the inclination shifts markedly. Giovanni di Simone was also the architect of the Monumental Cemetery and the church of Saint Francis, as well. He was killed in the dreadful defeat of the battle of Meloria and so never completed his work on the leaning tower. That defeat signalled the beginning of the decadence of the city and with it the work on the tower was slowed down. In the early years of the 14th century only the bell enclosure was still unfinished. In 1350 it was added by Tommaso Pisano, the third and final architect of the tower, which by then was already quite famous. It has now been scientifically proven that the tower leans due to the sinking of the terrain on which it stands.

It is an alluvial terrain of recent formation, hence soft, and is incapable of sustaining the heavy weight of the tower. And, in any case, many other buildings in Pisa also lean and this creates an extraordinary assemblage of palaces, churches, bell-towers and other buildings, all of them leaning in different directions.

The Italians love the tower of Pisa; it is one of the dearest symbols of their country.

The Leaning Tower still functions as the bell-tower of the Cathedral. The origins of bell-towers, considered typically Italian, derive from Arab minarets. Christians, centuries ago, in their travels were fascinated by the call of the muezzin who, from the tops of minarets, called the faithful to prayer. They imitated the minaret in the West, and especially in Italy. At the tops of the Byzantine towers of Ravenna, Florence, Rome, Pisa and many other cities they placed bells. As the muezzin still calls the people of Islam to prayer, and as this call is heard in the most arid, desolate areas of the desert under the burning sun, so the Italian bells carry out the same function, showing the path to God who is the same God for Italians, Arabs and all peoples.

The Leaning Tower, seen from the roof of the Cathedral. Probably the most famous tower in the world, it is renowned both for its architectural beauty and for its exceptional inclination.

Left
The entrance to the Leaning Tower.

Below
The inclination of the Tower is dramatized in this unusual view.

The sixth order of arcades and the belfry. The latter is ornamented by small arches, supported by corbels or small columns, which frame the openings. The belfry was completed in 1350 by Tommaso, the son of Andrea Pisano.

Far left
Detail of the blind arcade at the base of the Leaning Tower, with semi-columns and characteristic lozenge-shaped decorations.

Left
The terrace at the top of the tower can be reached by means of a 297-step spiral stairway.

45

THE BAPTISTRY

Diotisalvi began the construction of the Baptistry some years after having finished the small church of San Sepolcro. On two different pilasters of the Baptistry inscriptions which attest to that fact can still be seen. Thirty-four thousand families voluntarily paid a supplementary tax to continue the work which had suffered a long interruption. In 1278, the Baptistry was in part redone and the structural decoration was radically changed. A fresco of about 1385, depicts the Baptistry and the dome. Right after that period the Gothic decoration on the exterior was completed. The lack of stylistic continuity on the outside of the edifice is therefore justifiable. During the great restoration of 1841-56, the steps around the building were removed.

Grand and imposing, the Baptistry has a circumference of 107 meters and a total height of 54 meters. The building has a slight lean (45 cm.) toward the façade of the Cathedral. This lean may not be due to the sinking of the ground but rather to the original slope of the terrain on which the monument was built.

The main door of the Baptistry faces the Cathedral. Two beautiful columns of classical influence flank the door on either side, while in the building are two small ivory columns, reminiscent of Byzantine workmanship. In the eleven small panels to the right of the door are carved: *King David*, *Descent of Christ to Hell*, the *Twelve Apostles*, two *Angels* and the *Redeemer in Glory*. To the left are another eleven panels representing the symbols of the *Months of the Year* and the activities connected with them. September and October are combined into one panel. The architrave is carved in high relief with stories from the life of Saint John the Baptist, beginning with *Saint John Preaching*, the *Meeting of Saint John with Christ*, the *Meeting with Herod*, the *Baptism of Christ*, the *Dance of Salome*, the *Decapitation*, and finally the *Apostles who bury the body*. In the freize above the architrave are eleven small figures with Christ in the center, surrounded by the Virgin and Saint John, the four Evangelists and

four Angels. All these remarkable works show marked evidence of Byzantine influence.

The dome, on its eastern side, is divided into twelve sections which have been covered with lead and partially with tiles as well. The dome has small Gothic windows. At the top of this immense edifice is the statue of Saint John the Baptist. A work in bronze, it is about 3.30 meters in height. It was once attributed to Giambologna, but now it is believed to be by Turino di Santo (early part of the 15th century). Giovanni Pisano also worked in the Baptistry between the years 1277 and 1284.

Majestic and evocative, the interior of the Baptistry consists of a peristyle of four pilasters and eight columns. The extremely simple lines of the various styles unite harmoniously, both in the interior as well as the exterior of the building. The interior diameter of the Baptistry is 35.50 meters. No other Baptistry in Italy has dimensions which are so impressive. The first pilaster on the right, on entering the building, has an inscription which notes that the Baptistry was founded in August 1153. An inscription below that records the work of restoration between 1841 and 1856. The figures on the sculpted capitals are quite remarkable: they depict boar hunting, as well as animals and monsters. The baptismal font is most beautiful and is of octagonal form with four small basins. These small basins were for baptising babies in times when baptism, according to the rites of the Latin church, was by complete immersion. Adults were baptised in the large central basin. The panels of white Carrara marble which form the exquisite outer portion of the font have an oriental feeling and are delicate and very imaginative. An inscription on the inside of the font states that Guido Bigarelli da Como completed the basin in 1246. The only altar in the Baptistry was presented by Canon Gargino between the end of the 13th and the beginning of the next century, but it has been greatly restored. The altar is decorated with panels which are very si-

milar to those of the baptismal font. The floor, very much restored, is the work of artists from Como, students of the excellent Guido Bigarelli, who worked in Pisa in the 13th century.

The Pulpit in the Baptistry

Nicola Pisano built the pulpit in the Baptistry between 1255 and 1260. This work of the great Nicola marks a memorable date in the history of Italian sculpture and none of his later works are comparable in greatness. The sculptors who preceded him, Biduino, Gruamonte, Bonamico and all the others, are eclipsed by Nicola Pisano's marvelous achievement. Given the period in which it was created, the work of this great sculptor assumes the aspect of a true miracle. Fellow citizens of Nicola were so attached to the pulpit, that in the year 1303 an edict of the commune of Pisa ordered armed men to stand guard over it, in order to prevent any possible damage.

The pulpit, built with various marbles, has a hexagonal shape and is supported by six outer columns, three of which rest on the backs of lions, and by a central column with human and animal-like figures at the base. The striking lions bearing the lateral columns of the pulpit, and holding their prey between their claws, are especially to be noted. Of great interest rest are the small capitals and trilobate arches, which unite these capitals all the way around the pulpit. The small figures between the arches represent *Charity, Fortitude* (a beautiful, completely nude figure), *Humility, Fidelity, Innocence* and *Faith*. The upper part of the pulpit is composed of five panels which are separated by thin bands of small Gothic columns in red marble. The first panel depicts the *Nativity of Christ*, in which the Madonna shows obvious Etrusco-Roman influences. The second panel represents the *Adoration of the Magi*, where the classical references are even more accentuated; the Madonna is undoubtedly a copy of the majestic figure of Phædra on

Detail of the column to the left of the east door of the Baptistry: the reliefs on the door-jamb represent the months of the year.

Below
The figures on the upper part of the architrave over the main door of the Baptistry represent Christ, the Virgin and John the Baptist, with Angels and Evangelists. On the lower part of the architrave are episodes from the life of the Baptist.

the Roman sarcophagus at the Monumental Cemetery. The Adoration panel is probably the most significant of all the work of Nicola Pisano. The following scene is Child in this panel has been broken by unknown vandals. Most remarkable here is the high priest, in the act of accepting the Christ Child. The fourth and fifth panels are the *Crucifixion* and *Last Judgement*. These two works are truly notable, both for their composition and for the naturalism of the nude figures.
Notwithstanding the probable Apulian origin of Nicola, Tuscany was the triumphal ground of this great artist, and it was here that he came to dominate the entire field of Italian sculpture. In the works of Nicola Pisano all is force and energy. His limpid, powerful figures fill the spaces of his architectural structure, which no longer dominates the figures, but rather harmonize with them. Classical art inspired Nicola in his search for new expressive forms in the development of Italian sculpture. His open-mindedness, his artistic vision and his mode of expression were very controversial at the time. In his art, however, Nicola found his freedom, which signified then and still signifies today, the

The interior of the dome of the Baptistry.

Far left
This detail reveals the intense expression
of the face of the Madonna
by Giovanni Pisano, in the Baptistry.

Left
The Saint John the Evangelist
by Giovanni Pisano, together with
his Madonna and Child, have been
placed inside the Baptistry to protect
them from damage from bad weather.

freedom of Modern Man, restless and full of problems. He was not constricted by old medieval fears which looked back at the ancient classical world as something sinful and no longer adaptable to the reality of a different epoch. Nicola Pisano fought against the spirit of his time, and from the abyss of the darkest obscurantism a new man emerges, thanks to him, a man who looks with confidence to the future, dreaming of ever greater conquests to come.

Left

The baptismal font, the altar and the pulpit, seen from the women's gallery. The fonts where children are baptized by immersion can be clearly distinguished.

Below left

The baptismal font and (to the left) the pulpit. The font, by Guido Bigarelli, has a marble screen with central rosettes and geometric decorations. The statue of Saint John the Baptist which rises from the center of the font is by Italo Griselli (1929).

Below

A capital, from the interior of the Baptistry, with figures of animals and hunters.

Right

Partial view of the wide women's gallery of the Baptistry.

The pulpit of the Baptistry is Nicola Pisano's earliest work in Pisa (he finished it around 1260). The hexagonal shape of the pulpit is most probably derived from the shape of Castel del Monte, Frederick II's famous castle in Apulia, where Nicola seems to have received his first artistic training. The division of the sculptures into three levels reflects a complex cultural program: at the lower level, the lions and the other supporting figures symbolize natural forces; in the middle level, the Virtues and the Prophets symbolize spiritual forces; in the panels, the stories from the life of Christ represent historical time. Thus, for Nicola, everything merges into history, and we achieve the liberation from the immobile, anti-historical Byzantine forms and the renewal of classicism, rediscovered from the historical representations on the Roman sarcophagi. The intense dramatic quality of the relief panels, the perfect merger between the architectural and the sculptural structure, and the originality of the work, already Gothic but still with classical overtones, make the pulpit of the Baptistry one of the most important works of 13th-century art.

Details of the pulpit: the first two panels, representing the Nativity and the Adoration of the Magi.

Panels of the pulpit representing the Presentation in the Temple and the Crucifixion.

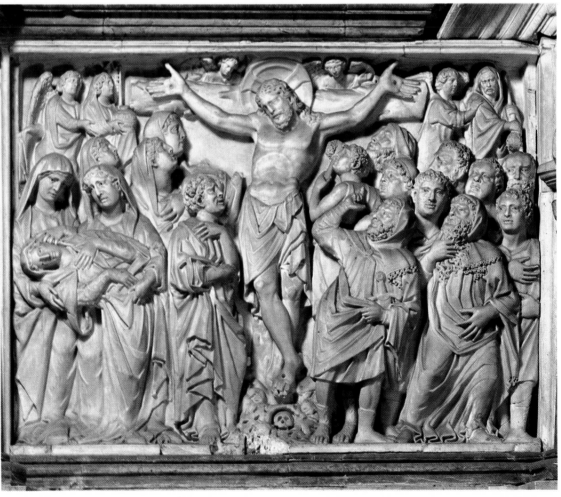

54

The panel of
the Last Judgement.

The Evangelist Matthew,
from the tympanum of the arch
under the panel of the
Last Judgement.

The **Damned**, detail of the panel of the Last Judgement.
The deformed, almost monstruous figures, a recurring feature
of Romanesque sculpture, are transformed in Nicola's art
into images of clear Greek and Roman derivation. Thus
the devils, beginning with the great Lucifer (to the extreme
right), are reminiscent of classical theatrical masks,
very common in ancient sculpture, but here enriched with a sense
of human tragedy, that same sense that fills all Nicola's work.

THE CAMPOSANTO MONUMENTALE

Facing the main portal of the Cemetery (Camposanto Monumentale), with the delicate Gothic workmanship of the Tabernacle, we can see a Latin epigraph on the left which states that the Monumental Cemetery of Pisa was begun in 1278, when Monsignor Federigo was Bishop of the city, Messer Tarlati was Podestà and Orlando Sardelli was in charge of the works. 'Johanne magistro edificante' was the very capable architect who today is known as Giovanni di Simone, builder of the Camposanto. There had once been a burial place around the Cathedral and the sepulchral inscriptions confirm this primitive and temporary Cemetery. In 1270 a new cemetery had been proposed, but it wasn't until three years later that the first definite decisions were taken. According to Giorgio Vasari, the greatest Renaissance art historian, the Cemetery at Pisa was completed in 1283, but this information has proved to be without foundation. It was just about that period that the work was interrupted because of the war against Genoa, and the subsequent defeat at Meloria. The work continued to drag on for decades. In 1358, for example, the foundations of the north wall had not yet been dug. At that period, only the south wall was completed with marbles and pilaster strips supporting the blind Byzantine arches. At the joining of these arches small heads were carved, each one different from the other. The previously mentioned Gothic tabernacle of the façade was, at first, attributed to Giovanni Pisano, but it was rather a late follower of his, perhaps Cellino di Nese, who completed the work in the second half of the 14th century. A Pisan legend has it that Archbishop Ubaldo Lanfranchi, commander of the Pisan armed forces during the Crusade called by Gregory VIII and Clement III, brought back from Palestine ships laden with earth from Golgotha, for the Cemetery of the Cathedral. This is still in the Cemetery area and is said to have the miraculous property of reducing bodies to skeletons in twenty-four hours. The inside of the Cemetery is formed by four long corridors. The plan is not perfectly symmetrical but the eye does not catch this irregularity. A sense of serenity and great peace dominates the entire edifice. Gauthier described the building as 'le plus beau Cimitière artistique du monde'. Franz Liszt was inspired and exalted on seeing the *Triumph of Death*. It was out of that inspiration that he composed the immortal *Toten Tanz* (Dance of Death).

The small graceful columns of the windows were added in stages, beginning with those of Lupo di Gante in the 14th century. But even in the 14th century and much later as well, these same windows were worked on by others, notably from the groups around Barbaresco and Ammannati. The chapel of the smaller eastern corridor was built in 1594, by the Archbishop Dal Pozzo, on the foundations of a pre-existing chapel.

The Cycle of Frescoes

Long before the Cemetery was completed it was decided to enrich it with pictorial decorations. In 1299, Vincino da Pistoia and Giovanni Apparecchiati executed for the church of the Cemetery a Virgin which is now lost. The great frescoes were undertaken in the second half of the 14th century, and were completed by Benozzo Gozzoli a century later. These were badly damaged during the last war. There are more than 600 tombs in the Cemetery belonging to medieval Pisan guilds and many others of famous families and other citizens. Through the centuries many ancient sarcophagi have been placed against the walls of the Cemetery and these are frequently used again as burial places. It was only at the end of the 18th century that burial, in general, in the Cemetery was stopped. However, even to our day, the most worthy, the most important sons of the city, as well as the most eminent scientists of the University of Pisa are laid to rest in the shade of the four cypresses, waiting for the perfumed roses of May to bloom in the cloister of the Cemetery.

The Triumph of Death

The *Triumph of Death* is a magnificent, strictly religious work of art and is the most famous fresco in the Cemetery. It was painted between 1338 and 1350 by an unknown master, although there have been frequent, discordant attributions. On the left, the hermit Saint Macarius is lecturing some important gentlemen on the vanity of life in the face of the disturbing, but true reality of the triumph of death. According to legend, the three open coffins contain the bodies of three Kings. Above and at the left, other hermit saints prepare for death while they spend their time in simple and earthly occupations. At the right, death is represented by a demonic figure, half woman, half devil. With scythe in hand the demon is ready to strike a group of young ladies and gentlemen. Death does not heed the call of those who await it as a liberation. The group of dead people belongs to every social condition, though for the most part they are persons who, notwithstanding their rank, are incapable of extricating themselves from their inevitable destiny. The babies coming out of the mouths of the dead represent the souls of the blessed and damned who are then dragged away by angels and demons, respectively.

It is obvious that the concept of the triumph of death was, in all probability, inspired by the Dominicans, such as, for example, Domenico Cavalca, the Blessed Giordano and Bartolomeo di San Concordio. The Dominicans, at that period, were in great favor in the city. It has been suggested that the magnificent painting of the *Triumph of Death* was painted after the plague of 1348. However, the concept of the triumph of death appreared frequently in religious literature. In the fresco the concept of death is expressed in all its dramaticity: a pressing reminder of the realities of life, that is that death can inexorably cut down any one of us of any social standing at any age or any moment. In the upper part to the right is the struggle between the angels and the demons over the various souls.

The Last Judgment

In the center of this other wonderful fresco are Christ on the right and the Virgin on the left, each portrayed within an almond-shaped background. On either side of them are the seated Apostles and, lower, a compact group of Archangels together with a majestic figure of the Archangel Michael. Sword in hand, he is intent on dividing the elect from the damned. At the left, we have the elect, ecstasy written on their faces, for they have been justly rewarded. In the serenity of the sublime moment, they gaze upward and pray to the Lord and the Virgin. The damned instead are filled with the most horrendous remorse and cry and lament because there is no repeal from their eternal condemnation. They have left all hope and are beginning the sentence of damnation; this is a warning to all, past and present, who look to their destiny with apprehension.

The tragedy of the damned has its natural fulfillment in the representation of Hell with the gigantic, horrible figure of Lucifer who seizes certain sinners with his teeth, among them Julian the Apostate, Nebuchadnezzar, and Attila. All around the 'emperor of the sorrowful kingdom' are the pits of hell for the damned, the heretics, the simoniacs, the slothful, the envious, the miserly and the lustful.

This fresco was greatly restored in 1378 by the painter Pietro da Pisa, in 1462 by Turino Vanni and in 1530 by the painter Sollazzino.

Thus the cycle of the triumph of death ends with an apocalyptic vision of Hell. The didactic-religious nature of the frescoes is very obvious. These realistic frescoes emphasize not only the tragedy and destiny of man but also his unceasing hope.

It is important to emphasize the unity of the entire cycle, which covers life, death, damnation and salvation; its stylistic quality, the pressing intensity of its allegories and the powerful expressionism, suggest the artist was probably not Tuscan, and Roberto Longhi has attributed the work to a Bolognese. But in any case, at least until new new evidence can provide us with the identity of this great artist, it is best to refer to him simply as the 'Master of the Triumph of Death'.

On the other hand, although it would be fascinating to be able to identify the artist with an already established painter, such as Orcagna or Traini (as unconvincingly has been done), his personality and his very rich and complex work is such that it does not need to be catalogued within our 14th-century art as the work of an already famous name. The artist belongs to the Tuscan or possibly Emilian post-Giotto culture, and his work is absolutely original despite the close ties with the art of the Lorenzetti brothers on the one hand, and of Orcagna and Traini on the other, which have often led to his identification with these artists.

Below

Interior of the Camposanto (Monumental Cemetery).

Right

The right doorway, or entrance, to the Camposanto.

Above

Detail, showing the capitals of the columns of the graceful four-light windows of the interior arcade in the Camposanto.

Right

The splendid Gothic tabernacle, over the entrance to the Camposanto, contains a Madonna and Child with Saints by the school of Giovanni Pisano.

Top
The northern wing of the open gallery of the Camposanto.

Above
This Roman sarcophagus of the 2nd century, with the story of Hippolytus and Phaedra, inspired various figures of Nicola Pisano's pulpit. The sarcophagus contains the remains of the Countess Beatrice, the mother of Matilde of Tuscany, and is housed in the northern wing of the Camposanto.

Right
Detail of the sarcophagus with the figure of Hippolytus.

Opposite
Panoramic view of the museum hall, behind the northern wing of the Camposanto, where the frescoes of the Triumph of Death, the Last Judgement, the History of the Anchorites and other works are exhibited.

The bronze Griffon, with the body of a lion and the head and wings of an eagle, is an Arabian work of the 10th-13th century. The Pisans took it as a trophy during the wars against the Saracens, and mounted it on the fastigium of the apse of the Cathedral.

The famous Madonna and Child by Giovanni Pisano, in the hall of the Triumph of Death.

The Emperor Henry VII with his
Counsellors, an outstanding work by Tino
di Camaino, from the funeral
monument in the Cathedral.

Opposite
Details of the fresco of the Triumph
of Death: young people playing music
in a woods; hunters on horseback
stopping before the three coffins of the

kings, while Saint Macarius warns them
about the vanity of human endeavor
when confronted with death.

Details of the Triumph of Death:
a noblewoman with her dog in a woods;
a lady with her dog in the riding party;
a hunter with his falcon
and his lady in a riding party.

Right

The Archangel Michael, detail of the
Last Judgement. This fresco is attributed
to the unknown author of the
Triumph of Death. Several names have
been suggested for this artist: Andrea
Orcagna, his brother, Nardo di Cione,
Pietro Lorenzetti, Francesco Traini,
Vitale da Bologna.

The Triumph of Death: detail of the Life of the Anchorites. The theme of the hermit's life is fairly common in 14th-century and early 15th-century painting, but here it must be interpreted as an integral part of the whole cycle, as a moment of calm in the midst of all the wild events of wordly life, as an idyllic interlude in the poem of vanity and pain, of death and damnation. The ability of this unknown painter in seizing and bringing together in a strange mixture of allegories the various aspects of life, is extraordinary. He also portrays the images of death, in a supreme form of allegory, which explain the very meaning of life and of the destiny of mankind.

The Last Judgement: detail of the Damned. It has been pointed out 'that in the variety of the light, at times gently flowing, at others harsh and cutting, the unknown painter seems to want to reflect the diversity of the things of this world' (Argan). Here the group of the damned, identifiable by their painful, masklike expression, form the dramatic moment, in contrast to the idyllic setting of the elect on the left of the fresco. It is important to emphasize once again that the meaning of the painting derives from its ideal and stylistic unity with the Triumph of Death: each scene is a metaphor and, all together, they attempt a definition of the meaning of existence.

The frescoes with episodes from the life of Saint Ranieri covered part of the southern wing of the Camposanto. They are almost entirely by the Florentine painter Andrea Bonaiuti, who executed the upper part around 1377, and by Antonio Veneziano, who painted the lower part between 1384 and 1388.
Antonio Veneziano: Saint Ranieri returning to Pisa. Detail of the head of the saint.
Andrea Bonaiuti: Detail of Saint Ranieri's Voyage to the Holy Land.

Left
Piero di Puccio: Eve. Detail of the Creation of Adam and Eve, originally in the northern wing of the Camposanto.

Below
Benozzo Gozzoli: David and Goliath. Remains of the fresco from the northern wing of the Camposanto.

Opposite, above
Spinello Aretino: The Conversion of Saint Ephisius. This fresco formed part of a cycle of episodes from the lives of Saints Ephisius and Potitus. It was composed in two rows, each containing three episodes, and was originally in the southern wing of the Camposanto.

Opposite, below
Spinello Aretino: detail of the Battle of Saint Ephisius against the Infidels.

The sinopite drawings for the frescoes in the Camposanto were discovered when the frescoes were removed from the walls.

Master of the Triumph of Death: Saint Macarius; noblewoman with her dog in the riding party; a saint from the Last Judgement.

Benozzo Gozzoli: sinopite drawings of two details of the Annunciation, originally above the entrance to the Ammannati chapel.

The pulpit of the Baptistry.

Sarcophagus of the Muses, in the Camposanto.

Detail of the Leaning Tower.

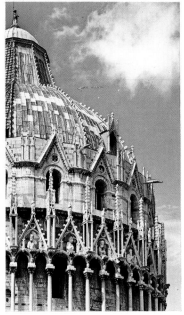

Detail of the Baptistry.

Sunset at the Piazza dei Miracoli.

Columns of the Leaning Tower.

The Cathedral seen from the Baptistry.

The Roman Lion Sarcophagus, in the Camposanto.

View of the Jewish Cemetery.

Bonanno Pisano: Herod.

The Cathedral and the Camposanto.

Polychrome decoration of the Cathedral.

The fastigium of the apse of the Cathedral.

The Eagle in the pulpit of the Baptistry.

The coffered ceiling of the Cathedral.

Hellenistic vase.

The Leaning Tower seen from the botanical gardens.

The door of Saint Ranieri.

THE NATIONAL MUSEUM OF SAN MATTEO

This museum has every right to be considered among the most important in Italy. It is situated in an old building on the Lungarno Mediceo and was originally a beautiful Benedictine Monastery. The monastery has undergone many architectural changes and has been used, through the centuries, also as a jail and even as a barracks.

The collection of great works now housed in the museum was begun in 1796, when Canon Zucchetti left a group of paintings to the Cathedral Museum. As time went on, through various gifts, this first nucleus grew until finally it gathered together an exceptional number of works of all periods which are fundamental in the history of art. At the end of the last century the collection was re-organized and transferred to the monastery of San Francesco. In 1949, after an extensive restoration of the old Benedictine Monastery, the art works were again on exhibition in the 37 halls of the new National Museum of San Matteo.

Among the many important works in the museum collection, the most worthy of note are particularly those of the best local artists (and by 'local' we mean to describe the artists' geographic origin and not to limit their importance). By Giovanni Pisano there are the *Dancing Figure* and the *Saint with a Reliquary*, the two splendid *Saints* from the Baptistry, and a small *Madonna*; by Giunta Pisano there is the wonderful *Crucifix*, certainly one of the most precious incunabula of Italian painting; by Andrea Pisano there is the *Virgin of the Annunciation* and by the Master of San Martino, a very important 13th-century artist, a *Madonna and Child*. The Master of San Martino is certainly one of the most interesting artists represented in the museum, since his work marks one of the high points of Pisan art, merging the aristocratic trends of Giunta with the more unsophisticated ones of Enrico di Tedice and with the novelties of the culture which surrounded him, such as the élitist classicism of Nicola Pisano. It can be said that this anonymous painter marks the end of the cycle of medieval painting in his city and, at the same time, begins the new epoch of Italian painting, expressed in Siena by the works of the predecessors of Duccio di Buoninsegna and by Duccio himself, and in Florence primarily by Cimabue, Giotto's teacher.

There are many other works of the same period (13th-14th century) by pupils and assistants of famous artists which give us a very varied and thorough idea of the art of the time, and especially sculpture. There are also some great works of this same period by artists who were not Pisans (in particular those from Siena), such as the *Madonna and Child with Saints* by Simone Martini and the *Annunciation* by Giovanni da Milano.

The early 15th century is represented first of all by a great masterpiece, the *Saint Paul* by the leader of the school of Renaissance painting, Masaccio; this panel is part of the *Polyptych* of the Carmine, now divided between London, Naples, Berlin and Vienna. The *Madonna and Child* by Gentile da Fabriano, although painted at the same time, is to be connected stylistically to the end of the late-Gothic period. We must also mention the *Redeemer* by Fra Angelico, and works by Ghirlandaio and Gozzoli.

We must not forget the works of later centuries which are also kept in the museum, such as *Rebecca at the Well* by one of the greatest Mannerist painters, Rosso Fiorentino; *Sacred and Profane Love* by Guido Reni; and lastly a very famous 'genre' painting, *The Flea*, by the Bolognese Giuseppe Maria Crespi. There are also many worthy examples of the minor arts, such as tapestries. It can be concluded that the National Museum of San Matteo is primarily important because of its collection of 13th and 14th-century Pisan art.

Cloister of the National Museum
of San Matteo.

The original refectory of the former
monastery contains a series of precious
polychrome statues, as well as the
masterpiece of Giunta Pisano.

Pisan artist of the 12th century: Crucifixion
with episodes from the life of Jesus.

This painted Cross, in tempera on wood, dates from the 13th
century and is by the school of Bonaventura Berlinghieri.

Right
Detail from the Crucifix by Giunta Pisano.

Opposite
Crucifix in tempera on wood by Giunta Pisano,
from the Church of San Ranierino.

Madonna and Child Enthroned, with episodes from
the life of the Virgin. This painting is considered the
masterpiece of Pisan painting of the 13th century.
The unknown artist has been named the Master of San Martino.

Right
This painting of Saint Anne and the Virgin
is also by the Master of San Martino.

This beautiful polyptych with the Madonna and Child and Saints is signed by Simone Martini, and was painted for the Church of Santa Caterina in 1320.

80

Saint Catherine, detail of the polyptych by Simone Martini.

Right
Altar frontal with Saint Dominic and episodes from his life, painted by Francesco Traini in 1344. It is in part a later copy. It was originally in the Church of Santa Caterina.

Below
Gentile da Fabriano: Adoration. A delicate work in typical late-Gothic style.

84

Guido Reni's Sacred and Profane Love is one of the
great Bolognese painter's most important works. Guido's
classicizing interpretation of Caravaggio's style can be noted
in the two mythological figures which emerge in a vivid flash
of light from the obscurity of the background.

Madonna and Saints by Giovanni Antonio Bassi,
called 'Sodoma'. Sodoma used the techniques of Leonardo's
'atmospheric' studies in accordance with his own hedonistic
taste for beautiful images, and
achieved an extreme refinement of form and color.

Left
Masaccio: Saint Paul. This panel is part of the great
polyptych painted in 1426 for the Church of the Carmine,
and later dismembered. Other panels are now in London,
Vienna, Berlin and Naples. The substantially human quality
of this image and the vitality of the masses which converge
in perspective (despite the old-fashioned gold ground
ordered by the patrons) reveal the truly revolutionary
significance of the work of the Florentine master.

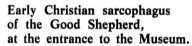

Early Christian sarcophagus
of the Good Shepherd,
at the entrance to the Museum.

Far left
Archangel with a Rose, perhaps by
Biduino da Bidogno (12th century),
from the tympanum of the Cathedral.

Left
Sculptured capital by Rainaldo,
from the façade of the Cathedral.

Below
Rainaldo: fragment of a column
with volutes and rosettes and
a graceful capital, originally
on the façade of the Cathedral.

Opposite
Christ Blessing, dated 1204 and
attributed to the master of the
architrave of the Baptistry door.
Originally part of the exterior
decoration of the Baptistry.

88

Opposite

Lion, Pisan art of the 13th century, originally at the main entrance to the Cathedral.

Giovanni Pisano: female figure known as 'The Dancer'.

Opposite, below

Decorative panel from the Cathedral, carved by a Pisan artist of the 13th century.

Above

The steps of the original exterior platform of the Cathedral were decorated in marble. These fragments, representing two dogs and a lion with the head of a woman, are by Giovanni Pisano.

The Virgin of the Annunciation, an elegant sculpture in polychromed wood by Andrea Pisano.

Female Head, by Nicola Pisano, from the exterior of the Baptistry.

Madonna and Child, a typical wood
sculpture of the French school
of the 13th century.

This painted terracotta bust
of the Redeemer has been
attributed to Verrocchio.

91

PIAZZA DEI CAVALIERI

Piazza dei Cavalieri (Square of the Knights) was the Roman 'forum' of the city where the two principal streets, the 'cardo' and the 'decumanus' intersected. At the time of the free republic of Pisa the piazza was called 'of the seven streets' because there was a confluence of seven streets. It was on this quiet square, full of historic memories, that in 1406 the Florentine Pier Capponi notified the people's representatives of Pisa that the independence of their glorious republic was at an end. The Sacred and Military Order of the Knights of Saint Stephen was founded in 1516 by the Grand Duke Cosimo I. At the same time he projected, on that piazza, all the buildings necessary to house the Order. There had been many medieval constructions on the piazza of 'the seven streets'. These were in such bad condition that it was impossible to restore them. Hence the decision to transform completely the piazza. In front of the Palazzo della Carovana the statue of Cosimo I was placed. It is a work of the Florentine sculptor Francavilla (1596), from designs by Giambologna.

The Church of the Knights

The Church of the Knights (Chiesa dei Cavalieri) was built in the same place where there had once been an older church called San Sebastiano delle Fabbriche Maggiori. Giorgio Vasari began the construction of the present building in 1565. The façade was not yet completed when the church was consecrated in 1569. Finally, between 1594 and 1606, the façade was finished and the result was a work of great elegance with the contrasting marbles of the columns, pilasters and decorations. Though the façade has been attributed to Bernardo Buontalenti, this does not correspond to the facts; the sole creator of the façade was actually Don Giovanni dei Medici.
The Grand Dukes Cosimo I and Ferdinando I, in an inscription at the top of the façade, are celebrated as the founders of the Order of the Knights of Saint Stephen, and also of this beautiful Renaissance church.
The two lateral naves were not part of

Vasari's simple design. They were added in 1682 by the architect Pier Francesco Silvani. The elegant bell-tower was built between 1570 and 1572, also on a design by Vasari.

The Interior of the Church

The interior of the church is full of works worthy of the strictest attention. To be noted, above all, are two holy water basins, the work of Carlo Fancelli, but on designs by Vasari. The pulpit built in 1627 is also the work of Fancelli, but it was originally created for the Cathedral which, in 1929-30, presented this magnificent work to the Church of the Knights. To the right and left of the entrance door are two impressive fragments of wood sculpture, pieces of an old galley of the Order, and above these flags captured from the Turks and from pirates by the brave Knights of Saint Stephen. At the center of the right wall, one can see another fragment of large dimensions which depicts arms, flags and slaves. It is probably the work of Santino, an excellent Pisan wood carver. At either end of the central nave there are two canvasses done in tempera and illustrating certain events in the life of Saint Stephen, patron saint of the Order. Another painting not to be overlooked is on the central door of the church; these are all attributed to Giorgio Vasari, rebuilder of the square and, therefore, of Renaissance Pisa. The ceiling made of precious woods is noteworthy. In the center of the ceiling there are many paintings, all dealing with the glorious achievements of the Order of Knights of Pisa. Cosimo III dei Medici had the main altar built. The Grand Duke had to wait a full nine years before he could see his magnificent altar completed. He also had to face the incredible cost of almost 20,000 'scudi' before it was completed. The altar, in oriental porphyry, was designed in 1682 by Pier Francesco Silvani. This original design was carried out in 1700 by Giovan Battista Foggini, but with certain modifications. The mortal remains of Saint Stephen, pope and martyr of the Christian

faith, have been placed in the urn on the altar. These were found in the cemetery of San Callisto at Rome. In the 12th century Saint Stephen's remains were taken to Trani, in far-off Puglia, but were later, at the insistence of the Grand Duke of Tuscany, transferred to Pisa in 1682. On either side above the main altar are two organs. The one at the left was built by the famous Sienese Azzolino della Ciaja following the model of the organs of Marseilles, Trent and Hamburg. In 1734 the organ was presented to the Medici Grand Duke, Gian Gastone, by della Ciaja and it was inaugurated at his funeral on November 28, 1737. After Napoleon's suppression of the Order of Saint Stephen, the organ suffered many alterations and it was only in 1914-15 that it was restored, with the addition of many stops and pipes taken from other celebrated organs. This magnificent creation of Azzolino della Ciaja is held to be a veritable masterpiece, and even today the organ of the Church of the Knights of Saint Stephen of Pisa is considered to be one of the best in all Italy, if not in the whole of Europe.

Palazzo della Carovana

Leaving the church, at the right, is the Palazzo della Carovana, or Palazzo degli Anziani, modernized in the 16th century by Giorgio Vasari for the Knights of Saint Stephen. This elegant building, in which the Knights took their course of instruction was called Palace of the Caravan (the word comes from the Persian and denotes: voyage, or navigation, in company). The motifs on the façade were likewise designed by Giorgio Vasari and were subsequently executed by his students.
With the passage of time these designs had been almost totally lost and so between 1902 and 1907 they were restored completely. On the upper part of the façade are the busts of six Medici Grand Dukes: Cosimo I, Ferdinando I, Francesco I, Cosimo II, Ferdinando II and Cosimo III.
In the square there are also other palaces.

Piazza dei Cavalieri, with the
Palazzo dei Cavalieri (also called
Palazzo della Carovana) and the
Church of Santo Stefano dei Cavalieri
(Church of the Knights).

The Palazzo dell'Orologio (or Palazzo
Gherardesca) was built for the Order
of the Knights of Saint Stephen at the
beginning of the 17th century, after
a design by Vasari. The central archway
connects the 'torre delle sette vie'
(the old prison) with the ruins
of the Gualandi tower,
where Count Ugolino was imprisoned.

Monument to Cosimo I dei Medici,
in front of the Palazzo della Carovana.

Below

The rich, coffered ceiling of the Church
of the Knights is splendidly
decorated with paintings commemorating
the feats of the knights. This detail,
by Jacopo da Empoli, represents
the conquest of Bona in 1607.

Opposite

Donatello, bust of San Rossore.
A precious reliquary in gilt bronze, in the
choir of the Church of the Knights.

among them that of the 'Orologio' (Clock)
built in 1607, again for the Order of Saint
Stephen. It is assumed that in this area
there had been a pre-existing medieval
building, the so-called Tower of the Gualandi, belonging first to the Commune of
Pisa and later to the Republic. A collection of eagles, as living symbols of the
Pisan Republic, were kept in the tower.
It was here that Count Ugolino in 1288,
accused of being the chief cause for the
catastrophe of the battle of Meloria, was
imprisoned, together with his sons and
grandsons. They were left to die of starva-
tion in that cursed tower. During the 17th
century this sinister building was incor-
porated into other edifices.

The Piazza dei Cavalieri has always been
one of the most beautiful and best propor-
tioned squares of Italy: the area has been
well planned mathematically and the resulting space has much elegance. This
square is the true historic center of a city
which, though no longer flourishing, is
still vital and keeps alive its traditions, its
past and unforgettable history.

OTHER PLACES OF ARTISTIC INTEREST

Santa Maria della Spina

The Chiesa della Spina (Church of the Thorn) was begun in 1323 by a master builder who has remained unidentified. In 1871, in order to prevent further infiltration of the waters of the Arno, the little church was taken apart, stone by stone, and rebuilt at street level. This relocation was the only way to guarantee the stability of the building. The outer decoration of Santa Maria della Spina was done by students of Giovanni Pisano. The rose window of the façade has been replaced with a modern copy. The side of the building on the Lungarno is more richly decorated and ornamented than the other sides. Especially, to be noted are the thirteen tabernacles, the Christ and the delicate small figures of Angels and Saints on the upper spires. On the west wall, in three different tabernacles, are sculptures depicting a Madonna and Child and three Saints. According to Giorgio Vasari, the model for one of the saints was Nicola, father of the author of the work, Giovanni Pisano. This was a rather affectionate tribute from the great son to his great father. In a small tabernacle in the church at one time there was a reliquary which, legend has it, contained a thorn from the crown of Jesus which was given to Betto Longhi by a Pisan merchant who had brought it from the East in 1333. The Grand Duke Ferdinand I put the Church of Santa Maria della Spina under the jurisdiction of the Hospital of Pisa, in this way making the hospital responsible for the maintenance of this most delicate building. The church of Santa Maria della Spina is undoubtedly a unique monument of Gothic architecture, and not only Italian. Its small size, the quality of its structure, and especially the richness of its decorations give the impression more of the work of a goldsmith, rather than an architect. It is almost as though its architect (who enlarged an existing oratory guarding a bridge) guessed that it would one day house one of the thorns of Christ's crown and deliberately made it look like a reliquary.

San Zeno

The Church of San Zeno dates back to at least the 10th century and was then connected to the Monastery of the Camaldolites. It is assumed that Pope Eugene III, who was of local origin, had been abbott of that monastery. The church of San Zeno was desecrated in 1809. Due to the many changes and modifications the building had suffered during the centuries, its basic architectural structure was hidden. After exceptional restorations, the old abbey of San Zeno has been brought back to its original architecture. Its columns and capitals, both Roman and Romanesque, have been entirely restored thanks to the effective work done by the Superintendence of Monuments and its most experienced architects.

San Pietro in Vinculis

Commonly known as San Pierino, this church was begun in 1074, exactly eleven years after work on the Cathedral had begun. It was consecrated in 1119 by Archbishop Pietro Moriconi.
In the Roman period, on the same spot where the Christian church now stands, there had been a pagan temple, dedicated to the god Apollo.
Most interesting are the windows above the doors and the architrave over the central door which is a classical imitation.
The interior of the church is divided into a nave with classical columns and capitals and round arches.
To the left of the church is the bell-tower, with arcades and windows giving on to the crypt. It was probably part of an older construction, transformed in the 11th or 12th century.

Santa Caterina

The Church of Santa Caterina (Saint Catherine) was built in the second half of the 13th century by the Dominicans. The façade was completed in 1327. The upper area of the façade has two rows of Gothic columns decorated with masks. Masks also encircle the rose window. The church has undergone many reconstructions and restorations, especially following the disastrous fire of 1651. The church has no aisles, but traces of an unfinished one are still visible. The slender bell-tower alongside the church is attributed to Giovanni di Simone and has undergone many changes, especially at the summit of the spire.
There are some splendid works of art in the church: the *Triumph of Saint Thomas*, by Traini; the funerary monument of Bishop Saltarelli by Nino and Andrea Pisano, as well as the monument to Gherardo Compagni; the sculptures of Nino Pisano; the *Madonna with Saints Peter and Paul* by Fra Bartolomeo.

San Michele in Borgo

According to tradition, this church, consecrated in 1040, was constructed on the ruins of a pre-existing pagan temple. The façade is late 14th-century and, in its upper section, has three rows of Gothic galleries with mask decorations. The interior has undergone much restoration and rebuilding. Traces of Byzantine frescoes are still visible.

San Paolo in Ripa d'Arno

The church, also known as 'the old Cathedral' was built in 805 for the Vallombrosians and underwent much rebuilding in the following centuries. Characteristics analogous to the Cathedral of Pisa can be seen on the admirable façade and the right side.
The façade has three rows of galleries of exquisite workmanship with some very fine columns.
The interior of the church is extremely severe and somber and has a remarkable trussed ceiling in wood.

The ancient Church of San Zeno has been restored
to its original structure. It contained many classical
and Christian sarcophagi, which were transferred
to the Camposanto in the last century.

The solemn and austere interior of San Zeno. The nave
and the aisles are separated by colonnades with rounded
and ogival arches; the capitals are Roman and Romanesque.

A Greek bas-relief representing three pairs of ears, to be found
in the Church of San Zeno. It is probably a reference
to the cult of the Alexandrine Triad which originated
in Egypt: it was a common belief of this cult
that the three gods listened to the prayers of mortals.

The Church of Santa Maria della Spina, considered the masterpiece of Pisan Gothic architecture.

The upper part of the façade is decorated with rose windows and rosettes. The graceful niches contain statues of the Madonna, Christ and Angels, by the schools of Giovanni and Nino Pisano.

Tabernacles and niches on the upper part of the right side of Santa Maria della Spina. The statues of Christ and the Apostles, on the upper part, are by the school of Giovanni Pisano; the statues on the pinnacles are from the workshop of Nino Pisano.

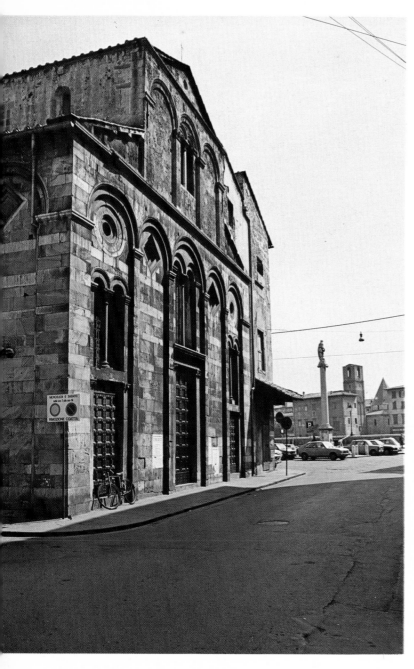

Façade of the Church of San Pietro in Vinculis,
with arcades and double-arched windows.

Interior of the Church of San Pietro. The three naves
are separated by arcades with interesting sculptured capitals.

Right
The crypt of the Church of San Pietro is divided by columns
and pilasters into four naves, and is covered by a cross-vault.

Opposite
The façade of the Church of San Paolo a Ripa d'Arno
dates from the beginning of the 13th century; it has
a high socle, in tufa, and grey and white marble facing.
The evolution of the sober Pisan style during the course
of the Romanesque period can be seen in the arcades,
and in the three orders of upper
galleries with arches of many forms and spiral columns.

The harmonious façade of the Church of San Michele in Borgo, completed by Fra' Guglielmo Agnelli, represents the transition from Romanesque style to Pisan Gothic.

The lower part of the façade of the Church of Santa Caterina, with Romanesque arcades, and, above, elaborate Gothic-style open galleries. The rose window was completed in modern times, although the reliefs, with busts of saints, date from the first half of the 14th century.

Nino Pisano: the Archangel Gabriel and the Virgin of the Annunciation. These two statues from the sides of the altar of Santa Caterina retain traces of the original color and gilding.

The Sinopia Museum in the Camposanto Monumentale

The Sinopia Museum of the frescoes in the Camposanto Monumentale is located in the old hospital of Pisa. It is important to remember that this hospital was founded following the defeat of the city by Pope Gregory IX. In the winter of 1240-1241 a ship coming from Provence with numerous prelates, bishops and cardinals aboard was going to Rome at the invitation of Pope Gregory IX in order to dethrone the great German Italian Emperor Frederick II Hohenstaufen. This ship was captured between the islands of Giglio and Montecristo and the bishops and cardinals were taken in chains as prisoners to Pisa by the faithful allies of Emperor Frederick. When this became known in Rome, the irate Pope immediately excommunicated the Ghibelline city and all of its inhabitants. When Alexander IV became pope several years later, Pisa was pardoned through a pontifical decree dated 13 March 1257 on the condition that the Pisans build a hospital at their own expense.

At that time the Bishop of Pisa was Federico Visconti, contemporary and protector of the greatest of the Pisano sculptors, Nicola, who expressed the best of his art in the representation of the neo-classical world adapted to a Christian doctrine. The pardon which Pisa received from Rome was very probably a result of the intercession of Federico Visconti. However, the Pisans complained about the expenses which they had to sustain and the polemic ended only when they finally placed the first stone, on the day of Pentecost 1257, of what was to become the present day Hospital of Santa Chiara, on the south side of the Piazza del Duomo. The construction was practically finished in 1286. Between 1336 and 1337 the building was definitively completed on the south side of the Piazza del Duomo. Naturally the building changed over the centuries and especially in 1830-1832 when the decorations by Coluccio da Lucca (1338) were restored. The old hospital of Pisa was restructured in 1979 by the architects Gaetano Nencini and Giovanna Piancastelli in order to house the sinopias.

Sinopias are preparatory drawings traced directly on to the wall which has been covered by a special plaster base called 'arriccio'. This technique was used by artists who undertook to paint large frescoes because of a lack of sufficient quantities of paper or other portable material.

Why were the preliminary drawings for frescoes called sinopias? The name derives from the city of Sinope, in Syria, where the red pigment used for these comes from. (We also find some sinopias either drawn or highlighted in green, yellow or black pigments). Once the artist had drawn his sketch, he would cover a part of this with a heavier type of plaster, richer in lime, called grassello; he would then fresco the prepared surface and continue in this way until the whole of the surface had been covered. The sinopias were therefore destined to disappear forever. In the case of the Monumental Cemetery in Pisa these were discovered and saved through unfortunate circumstances. During the battle of the Arno during the last war, a fire resulting from the explosion of a cannon in the Camposanto caused the destruction of some parts of the frescoes and rendered others so delicate that it became necessary to detach them. The great sinopias reemerged from beneath the detached frescoes and after complex restoration procedures were placed in this Museum. These are the most extensive existing documents of 14th and 15th century drawings where we can admire the genius of some of the greatest artists of that period. To give some practical indications, we suggest that the visitor go at once to the first floor where he can admire the panels depicting the stories of the Fathers of the Church, the Last Judgement, Hell and the Triumph of Death. Their composition is witness to the genius of an artist who was fundamental to the development of Italian art in the 14th century. There have been long debates in order to try and establish his identity and often the conventional name of 'The Master of the Triumph of Death' has been cited. In 1974 Luciano Bellosi attributed the frescoes to Buonamico Buffalmacco, a painter of the early 14th century and a pupil of Andrea da Tafo who was one of the principal artists in the decoration of the ceiling of the Baptistery in Florence.

Next to the work of Buffalmacco the visitor can admire a marvelous representation of the Crucifixion. This must have been the first sinopia in the Camposanto, probably drawn around 1320-1330 by Francesco Traini, the Pisan artist of European importance. He was influenced by the works of Lippo Memmi and especially by those of the great Sienese artist Simone Martini but his work is also an expression of personal originality.

From the first floor looking towards the Piazza the visitor can admire two rows of somewhat smaller sinopias, attached to two long panels. These are the work of Taddeo Gaddi, Andrea Bonaiuti, Antonio Veneziano and Spinello Aretino, four masters who worked in Florence during the 15th century. Taddeo Gaddi, Giotto's favourite pupil, was known to his contemporaries for his research on perspective; Andrea Bonaiuti produced some of the most magnificent compositions of this period and Antonio Veneziano succeeded in blending the Giottesque and Bolognese artistic traditions. Towards the end of the 14th century and the beginning of the 15th century Spinello Aretino revived the Giottesque tradition, filling his scenes with liveliness and colour.

Still on the same floor we can see the immense sinopia of the Theological Cosmography by Piero di Puccio from Orvieto and others by the same artist depicting the Coronation of the Virgin and the first chapters of Genesis.

The works in the Camposanto and the sinopias in the Museum are the only known works by Piero di Puccio from Orvieto but they are more than sufficient to give us an idea of this remarkable creator of architectural forms in space, most attentive to proportional rhythms and an inventor of extraordinary perspectival experiments.

Sinopias by Benozzo Gozzoli, or Benozzo di Lese as he is known, are on the ground floor. At the time of Benozzo, the availability of paper made the integral sinopia drawing on the wall unnecessary. The designs were first made on paper, then transposed onto the wall piece by piece. On the one hand, Benozzo's sinopias reveal the rigorous mathematical system which he followed in order to construct his perspectives; and on the other they reveal a multitude of small details, often joking in character, which testify to the variety of interests which occupied the master and his pupils each day on the scaffolding prepared for them so that they could do their painting.

Anyone who wishes to have an idea of the fresco cycle before the terrible destruction of 1944 can go out onto the walkway fixed to the side nearest the Piazza. The engravings done by Carlo Lasinio and coloured by his son Gianpaolo at the beginning of the 19th century give a vivid idea of what can be considered the most extensive cycle of 14th and 15th century frescoes.

The Church of San Sepolcro, by Diotisalvi.

Lunette from the Church of San Sepolcro.

The Church of San Martino.

The Church of San Frediano.

A relief from the Church of San Martino.

The Church of San Matteo.

The chapel of Saint Agatha.

The portico of the Church of San Zeno.

The Church of San Paolo a Ripa d'Arno.

Participants in the Palio.

Boat race on the Arno.

The end of the traditional contest, or Palio.

The old fortress, or citadel.

Galileo, portrait by Sustermans.

The courtyard of the University.

The fountain in Piazza dei Cavalieri.

Piazza delle Vettovaglie with its market.

Sunset at the mouth of the Arno.

Silhouettes at sunset of the Church of Santa Maria della Spina and the Guelph Tower in the citadel. The latter was built by the Florentines immediately after the occupation of Pisa.